THE LEROY ANDER

SONGBOOK · A CENTENNIAL CELEBRATION

Alfred Publishing Co., Inc. wishes to thank the Leroy Anderson Family and Woodbury Music Company for providing photographs, memorabilia, and original manuscripts for this songbook.

www.leroy-anderson.com

All images courtesy the Leroy Anderson Family, except as noted.

Alfred

Alfred Publishing Co., Inc.
16320 Roscoe Blvd., Suite 100
P.O. Box 10003
Van Nuys, CA 91410-0003
alfred.com

ISBN-10: 0-7390-5046-X
ISBN-13: 978-0-7390-5046-0

Leroy Anderson

An arranger, orchestrator, musician, conductor, and songwriter, Leroy Anderson (1908–1975) is best known for writing the holiday staple "Sleigh Ride," which is included in this collection. Along with dozens of other so-called "light classical" favorites, the works of this modest man from Cambridge, Massachusetts, have had a prodigious effect on American popular music. Very few individuals can be credited with inventing a particular style of music, but Anderson's highly innovative, infectious, and delightful "pops miniatures" combined classical and popular music in a way that had not been done until he arrived on the scene in the 1930s.

Anderson in the 1960s.

Although better known as a composer of instrumental works, Anderson initially wrote lyrics as well. In the early 1950s, Anderson collaborated with lyricist Mitchell Parish to produce vocal versions of seven of his best-known compositions. In fact, if it weren't for Parish's lyrics, "Sleigh Ride" would most likely not be ranked alongside "White Christmas," "Silent Night," and "Jingle Bells" as one of the most familiar and beloved songs performed during the Christmas season.

In commemorating the centennial of Anderson's birth, Alfred Publishing has assembled 33 of Anderson's songs for this collection. Included are all seven songs combining Anderson's melodies with Mitchell Parish's lyrics plus songs from Anderson's one and only Broadway musical, the 1958 production of *Goldilocks.* As an added "bonus," two previously unpublished songs are included that Anderson wrote toward the beginning of his career, along with one song from an abandoned musical based on the Civil War saga *Gone With the Wind.*

Early Years

Franklin Leroy (pronounced "luh-ROY") Anderson was born in Cambridge, Massachusetts on June 29, 1908, to Swedish immigrants who had arrived in America in the late 19th century. Both of Leroy's parents were musical; his father sang and played mandolin while his mother played organ at a Covenant church near their home. Young Leroy enjoyed the folk songs his family brought over from Sweden as well as popular music of the day. Much of the latter he picked up from listening to radio, which was first becoming prevalent in the 1920s.

Bror and Anna Anderson with their two children, Franklin Leroy (standing) and Russell (seated).

While growing up, Anderson learned a variety of instruments, including piano, organ, string bass, tuba, and trombone, the latter instrument as the result of his father's desire to see his son play someday in the Harvard University Band. Anderson's gift for arranging and orchestrating came early, and by the time he entered Harvard as a freshman in 1925, he had already begun writing music, having composed, orchestrated, and conducted his high school class song.

Anderson as a trombone student at Harvard.

It was at Harvard that Anderson's musical talents began to blossom. A music major, Anderson worked with each member of the faculty, including famed Roumanian composer Georges Enesco, who spent time as a composer-in-residence. Most influential of all, however, was American composer Walter Piston, a recent Harvard graduate who joined the faculty in 1926. The prevailing direction American composers were taking in the 1920s was toward radically dissonant and atonal music, as evidenced by works of Stravinsky and Schoenberg, among others; however, Anderson's tendency at Harvard toward writing strictly melodic works reflected a sensibility better approaching that of Tin Pan Alley songwriting than contemporary classical music. Satisfying his father's wishes, Anderson joined the Harvard band as a trombonist, eventually becoming its musical director.

HARVARD UNIVERSITY BAND
H
HARVARD UNIVERSITY BAND
H

Leading the Harvard University Band, 1929.

After earning his B.A. in 1929, he was elected to Phi Beta Kappa, which was followed by receipt of his master's degree. Anderson's continued association with the Harvard band, however, resulted in rejections of his applications for the Paine Traveling Fellowship, which would have allowed him to pursue further studies in Europe. According to the chairman of Harvard's music department, the band was not deemed to be a "proper" organization for a serious music scholar. As a result, Anderson enrolled in Harvard's Ph.D. program, concentrating on German and Scandinavian languages. He would become fluent in seven languages, a talent that would come in handy later, during the war years.

Arthur Fiedler and the Boston Pops

In 1936, George Judd, manager of the Boston Symphony Orchestra and a Harvard graduate himself, asked Anderson to write a medley of Harvard songs that would be performed by the Boston Pops Orchestra on its annual Harvard Night. The Boston Pops had been created in 1885 to entertain summer audiences after the regular season of the Boston Symphony had concluded. Consisting of musicians from the Boston Symphony excepting the first chair players, the Pops enabled the musicians to have year-round employment. The repertoire of the Pops was decidedly lighter, with Strauss waltzes, tone poems, and excerpts from well-known works presented. Beginning in 1930, the conductor of the Pops was Arthur Fiedler (1894–1979), whose desire to expose classical music to a wider audience led to his becoming the most successful proponent of these more accessible styles.

Anderson and Arthur Fiedler before a 1954 Boston Pops concert, at the 25th reunion of Anderson's Harvard Class of 1929.

Anderson himself was invited to lead the Pops in the medley, which he called "Harvard Fantasy." On the night of June 16, 1936, the exuberant response to Anderson's work led to Fiedler inviting him to compose short *aperitifs* that the orchestra could perform. The result was Anderson's first published work, "Jazz Pizzicato," in 1938. *Pizzicato*, the term used to indicate the plucking of the strings with one's fingers, had been used by several composers in writing entertaining encores.

Most notable of these include the "Pizzicato Polka" by Leo Delibes and the "Playful Pizzicato" movement of the *Simple Symphony* by Benjamin Britten. "Jazz Pizzicato" showed Leroy Anderson combining, for the first time, elements of classical and popular music in an attempt to reach a wider audience. The piece is performed entirely in the pizzicato style by each instrument in the string section of the orchestra, which includes the violins, violas, cellos, and basses. Although "Jazz Pizzicato" is far from being jazz, or even jazzy, it does incorporate syncopated rhythms that imply something more audience friendly than the classical works symphony orchestras usually performed.

In uniform during World War II.

Leroy Anderson Conducts

In 1942, Anderson entered the military, utilizing his knowledge of languages by serving overseas in Military Intelligence, translating pertinent written material into English. He was especially valuable for his expertise in the Icelandic language. When he was released in 1946, he returned immediately to his composing. Arthur Fiedler recognized Anderson's talent for creating melodic, attractive pieces that would be accessible to young and old listeners alike, regardless of their experience with classical music. In addition, Anderson's works were wonderfully self-descriptive, and often reflected musical versions of images that most people could relate to. Eventually, Fiedler would premiere many of Anderson's new compositions, which, over the next few years, included "The Syncopated Clock" (1945), "Fiddle-Faddle" (1947), "Serenata" (1947), "Saraband" (1948), and "Sleigh Ride" (1948).

What few people (including the composer himself) realized was that Leroy Anderson was creating an entirely new genre of music. Each composition was extremely well crafted, impeccably arranged and thought out, and, for all its airiness, deceivingly sophisticated. Anderson's works would eventually represent adjectives that described post-war America: optimistic, cheerful, innovative, whimsical, carefree, and infectious. Melodies were instantly memorable. Rhythms reflected onomatopoeic sounds, and Anderson's later works would take this one step further, employing a variety of sound effects in many of his most popular songs, including typewriters ("The Typewriter"), meowing cats ("The Waltzing Cat"), sandpaper ("Sandpaper Ballet"), ticking clocks ("The Syncopated Clock"), the clip-clopping of horses ("Horse and Buggy"), and even the sound created by musicians rubbing their hands on their instruments (used in another pizzicato tour de force, "Plink, Plank, Plunk!"). The result enabled classical music to break through age, economic, and educational barriers. Many children, initially attracted by the so-called novelty devices used by Anderson, were ushered into the world of the symphony orchestra, and thus, classical music, thanks to Leroy Anderson.

Late 1940s portrait.

Anderson in a jovial mood, 1950s.

Through Anderson's music, people began to realize that classical music didn't have to be boring, stodgy, lengthy, and humorless. Leroy Anderson had become classical music's first crossover artist, conquering the popular as well as the classical worlds. In time, other composers tried to emulate Anderson's success, including Percy Faith, Frank Perkins, David Rose, and Robert Farnon, triggering a mini-industry of light instrumental semi-classical music that would flourish for decades. Anderson was often asked how he came up with ideas for his songs. His usual answer was that he was in a constant state of alertness, being able to recognize song ideas when they came to him. In a 1970 interview, Anderson added to this point by saying the problem he faced was not in coming

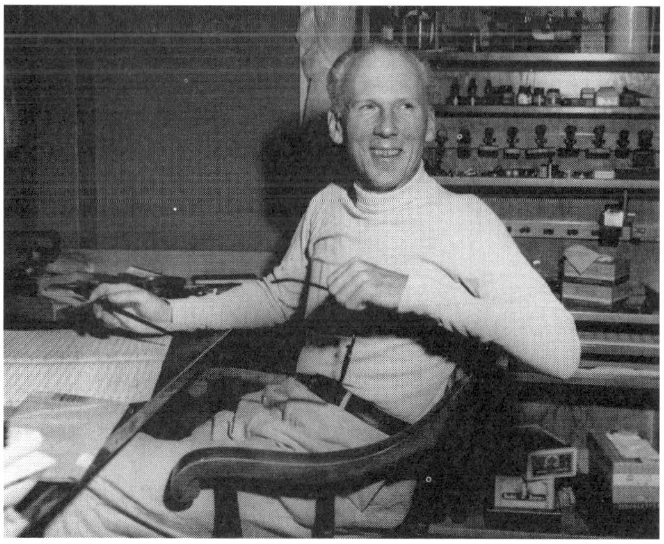

Anderson at home in 1952.

up with ideas, but differentiating between good ideas and bad ideas, and throwing the bad ones out before wasting any time developing them.

The concept of using symphonic instrumentation and classical works for consumption by the mainstream record-buying public was nothing new. During World War II, many popular songs were fashioned by adapting melodies drawn from longer classical works, such as Frank Sinatra's recording of "Full Moon and Empty Arms," the melody of which was taken from Rachmaninoff's second piano concerto, and Freddy Martin's "Tonight We Love," which was adapted from Tchaikovsky's first piano concerto. Leroy Anderson's works took this one step further, as he invented melodies that rivaled the most memorable works of Beethoven, Tchaikovsky, and Johann Strauss, Jr., but with an eye toward the popular rather than the classical market.

Rehearsing for a recording session, early 1950s.

With the success of "Fiddle-Faddle" in 1947, Anderson began to be nationally known for his contributions to the Boston Pops' repertoire. Realizing how popular his music was becoming, Decca Records invited Anderson to record his compositions with his own 50-piece studio group, dubbed the "Pops" Concert Orchestra. Many of the musicians were members of the New York Philharmonic, which was on hiatus. Beginning with two 10-inch LPs (long playing records), "Leroy Anderson Conducts His Own Compositions" (DL-7509) in 1950, and "Leroy Anderson Conducts His Own Compositions, Volume II" (DL-7519) in 1951, Anderson became a star on his own, a fact that made the publicity-conscious Arthur Fiedler envious (and a little bit resentful) of Anderson's growing celebrity status.

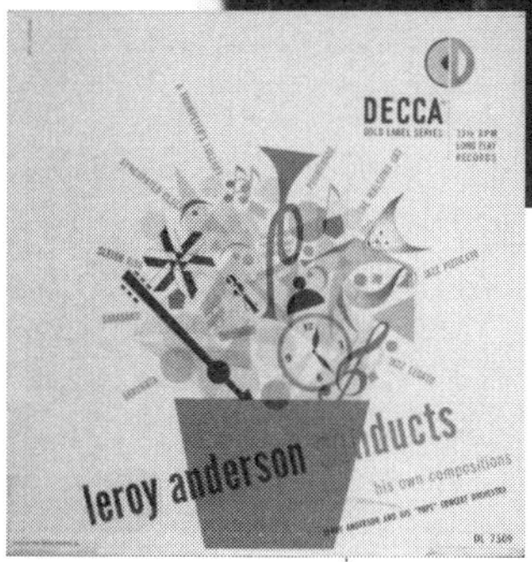
DECCA

Leroy Anderson's first long-playing record, 1950.

The brevity of Anderson's "pops miniatures," as they began to be called, was ingeniously appropriate for the record business at mid-century. The industry was in the midst of the so-called "speed wars," during which the reign of the 78 rpm record was being challenged by two new innovations: Columbia's LP record, which played at 33 1/3 rpm, and RCA Victor's 45 rpm "single." The LP, which was introduced in 1948, was created mainly for consumers of classical music, who were tired of having to constantly flip fragile 78 rpm records, which had a capacity of three to four minutes of music per side. With the LP, a listener could hear up to 20 minutes of uninterrupted music without having to get up to change the record. The 45, which was introduced in 1949, was created for the pop market; a more compact, more durable method of playing pop songs, which generally were three minutes in length or less. Leroy Anderson's songs satisfied fans of both formats; they purchased LPs that contained eight of Anderson's songs as well as 45 singles that contained one complete song on each side. The most logical next step in Anderson's march toward popular music respectability was to include lyrics. Enter Mitchell Parish.

Mitchell Parish

It was Anderson's publisher, Jack Mills, who came up with the idea to apply lyrics to a selection of Leroy Anderson's instrumental compositions, eyeing increased sales from the popular music market. When Mills asked Anderson his permission to do so, the composer was initially reluctant, fearing that any vocal editions of his songs might supersede his meticulously crafted orchestrations in popularity; however, when Mills brought up the name of Mitchell Parish, Anderson changed his mind and agreed to the proposal.

© Photofest

Mitchell Parish, lyricist for seven of Anderson's compositions, including "Sleigh Ride," 1950s.

Mitchell Parish (1900–1993) was an anomaly in the world of popular music songwriting, a specialist who wrote lyrics for established instrumentals and also provided English lyrics for foreign hits. With a few exceptions (such as Irving Berlin and Cole Porter), popular songs were written by teams of writers, with one responsible for the music and the other for the lyrics. Songs would be crafted concurrently, with the partners working together to come up with the final product. Parish was a hired gun who was brought in to fashion lyrics for an existing instrumental, often years after the original had been written, sometimes even changing the song title itself in the process. During his career, Parish had been incredibly successful, contributing lyrics to classic songs such as "Star Dust," "Sweet Lorraine," "Sophisticated Lady," "Stars Fell on Alabama," and "Moonlight Serenade." To Jack Mills, the melodic hooks of Leroy Anderson's songs were perfect for Parish to work with, and in 1950, Parish began writing lyrics for some of Anderson's more popular instrumentals.

One problem faced by Parish was that he was restricted, because Anderson's melodies and song titles had already been defined; thus, he had to work within those parameters, unlike the typical composer/lyricist relationship, where changes could be made as the songs were written. In 1970, Anderson told an interviewer that he and Parish collaborated closely on most of his work. Parish would ask Anderson questions concerning stress and accent and then make lyric suggestions, which Anderson would approve. In some cases, Anderson would recommend specific lyrics himself, whereby Parish would place them in the proper position within the song. Despite his initial misgivings, Anderson was pleased with the final results. The first two songs to get the Parish treatment were "The Syncopated Clock" and "Sleigh Ride."

Original sheet music edition of the vocal version of "Sleigh Ride," 1950.

SLEIGH RIDE
Words by MITCHELL PARISH Music by LEROY ANDERSON
Mills Music

First published in 1945, "The Syncopated Clock," which used temple blocks to represent the ticking of the clock in the title, was recorded as an instrumental by Leroy Anderson and his "Pops" Concert Orchestra in 1950. A version recorded by Percy Faith and his Orchestra in 1951 was adopted by WCBS-TV in New York as the theme song for its nightly cavalcade of motion pictures titled *The Late Show.* Despite a modestly successful vocal version recorded by Rosemary Clooney, the ever presence of the Faith recording, heard on television on a nightly basis for the next 25 years, made that version the more popular with the public.

Parish's lyrics for "Sleigh Ride" were a different matter altogether. The idea for "Sleigh Ride" had come to Anderson during a heat wave in 1946 while he was digging trenches at his summer cottage in Woodbury, Connecticut. The sounds of sleigh bells and the rhythmic galloping of horses' hooves were vividly presented in Anderson's composition, which became popular when it was first performed by the Boston Pops in 1948. The Pops had the first recording of the work in 1949, with Anderson's own "Pops Concert" recording following in 1950. Parish's lyrics, however, elevated the song from just another Anderson miniature to a holiday classic. The words fit the melody perfectly, projecting a joyous, festive image many associate with the Christmas season, despite the fact that the lyrics are merely seasonal and do not mention Christmas at all. In addition, Parish included onomatopoeic lyrics of his own, with words like "giddy-yap" and "ring ting tingle-ing" matching the rhythm of Anderson's melody. Vocal recordings of "Sleigh Ride" popped up almost immediately, with a version by the Andrews Sisters (Decca) arriving in time for the 1950 holiday season. Since that time, "Sleigh Ride" has become Anderson's most popular composition, with vocal versions recorded by artists ranging from Garth Brooks and James Brown to Neil Diamond and Bing Crosby. Today it ranks in the upper tier of the most popular holiday songs ever written.

Anderson displays the "slap-stick" and sleigh bells used in "Sleigh Ride."

In 1952, Anderson's recording of "Blue Tango" crashed through the pop barrier, selling two million copies and becoming a gigantic hit, becoming the first instrumental to make it to No.1 on the Hit Parade and topping the *Billboard* pop charts for five weeks. Exotic rhythms were all the rage in pop music, which was still trying to find its way after the demise of the big band era in the late 1940s. The radio airwaves and jukeboxes were filled with records featuring rhumbas, cha-chas, and mambos. Anderson's infectious combination of the tango with occasional "blue" (flatted) notes became the biggest-selling record of the year and one of the most-covered compositions of the decade. Although Parish's lyrics were recorded by Gisele Mackenzie and Nelson Eddy, Anderson's instrumental version became the one most familiar to the record-buying public.

leroy anderson conducts
DECCA
blue
tango
and other favorites

1954 Decca LP

Between 1950 and 1962, Mitchell Parish would pen lyrics to four other Anderson instrumentals. In "Serenata," Parish brought forth the image of a Spanish-flavored romantic interlude, with a handsome suitor serenading his *amour* from beneath her window. Anderson was always fond of the vocal rendition of the song as recorded by jazz singer Sarah Vaughan.

The song title "Belle of the Ball" lent itself perfectly to its breezy 3/4 waltz tempo, with Parish's lyrics romantically describing the carefree magnetism of an exquisitely beautiful girl who is the object of everyone's desire who sees her.

Anderson's impeccable and evocative orchestration made it easy for Parish to provide lyrics for "The Waltzing Cat," with the word "meow" used to accompany the swooping glissandos of the violins. In order to set up the premise of the meowing dancing cat, however, Parish added an introduction, with Anderson providing the melody. The final Anderson/Parish collaboration was "Forgotten Dreams," the lyrics of which were published in 1962. Parish's words brought forth a feeling of wistful nostalgia for a lost love, as exemplified by Anderson's simple but eloquent melody (which Anderson played on the piano himself in his recording of the song).

Belle of the Ball
The Waltzing Cat

Original sheet music editions featuring Mitchell Parish's lyrics.

Goldilocks

By the late 1950s, Leroy Anderson had devoted nearly all of his time to composing his pops concert miniatures, performing them in concert, and recording them with his own orchestra. There were other avenues in the industry where Anderson would most likely have excelled as well; however, for whatever reason, he never pursued them. One of these was in film music. Some of the industry's most honored and accomplished composers worked primarily in film, such as Miklós Rózsa, Franz Waxman, Max Steiner, Alex North, and Bernard Herrmann, among many others. With Anderson's gift for writing image-evoking melodies and masterful orchestrations, he would have been a natural for thc gcnrc. He also could have emulated the work of Carl Stalling by becoming a composer for animated cartoons, a field that, without doubt, would have been financially lucrative.

Another genre, which Anderson had aspired towards for most of his life, was the musical theater. As a fan of icons such as Richard Rodgers and Jerome Kern, one of Anderson's greatest desires was to score a Broadway musical comedy. In the late 1940s, an opportunity presented itself when he was asked to write the score for a show based on the *My Sister Eileen* series of short stories written by Ruth McKenney and published in *The New Yorker* magazine, with lyrics provided by Arnold B. Horwitt. Anderson and Horwitt's score was rejected, however, and the project, now titled *Wonderful Town*, was turned over to composing wünderkind Leonard Bernstein and the lyric-writing team of Betty Comden and Adolph Green. The show eventually became a huge hit on Broadway in 1953.

© *Photofest*
Walter and Jean Kerr during rehearsals for *Goldilocks*, c. 1958-59.

Despite this setback, Anderson still had his eye on writing for Broadway, avidly consuming every musical that came to New York, learning their songs, and buying the cast albums as they came out. In 1958, Anderson was approached by Walter Kerr, a famous theater critic who wrote for the *New York Herald Tribune*, who was, with his wife, Jean, preparing a satire of the silent movie industry to be titled *Goldilocks*. The Kerrs were no Broadway novices; Walter had written and directed the 1944 Broadway musical *Sing Out, Sweet Land*, a tribute to America's indigenous folk songs, and provided material with his wife for the 1949 revue *Touch and Go* as well as *The Vamp* in 1955, the latter show also dealing with the silent screen era. In addition, Jean Kerr had penned a best-selling novel, *Please Don't Eat the Daisies*, a book based on the Kerrs' suburban life in Larchmont, New York.

Walter Kerr had been a fan of silent movies ever since his boyhood days growing up in Evanston, Illinois. He believed that the glory days of knockabout slapstick comedy was best personified by the Mack Sennett Comedies Corporation, producers of shorts that specialized in frantic car chases (many featuring the Keystone Cops) and pie-in-the-face warfare. As a well-known and highly successful composer all during the 1950s, Leroy Anderson was a natural choice for the Kerrs to write the music for their play.

Jean Kerr
Walter Kerr
Goldilocks
A PLAY

Original *Goldilocks* play, 1958.

The plot for *Goldilocks* revolved around the tumultuous relationship between a tight-fisted, devious movie mogul and his sardonic leading lady at the Fort Lee, New Jersey, movie colony in 1913. The role of movie producer Max Grady was initially given to Ben Gazzara, but Gazzara, having no musical experience on the stage, bowed out before rehearsals began. Walter Kerr then chose Barry Sullivan to replace him. During tryouts in Philadelphia, it was determined that Sullivan, too, could not sing, and he gracefully withdrew from the production. Kerr's next choice was Don Ameche, a dashing leading man who not only had a good singing voice, but was adept at comedy as well. Ameche replaced Sullivan during thc show's run in Boston. To play the acid-tongued actress Maggie Harris, Kerr selected Elaine Stritch, who had starred in the national touring company version of *Call Me Madam*, playing the role Ethel Merman memorialized on Broadway.

© Photofest

Don Ameche as Max Grady and Elaine Stritch as Maggie Harris, 1958.

The score was vintage Anderson. Memorable melodies abounded, and Anderson captured the essence of the nascent motion picture industry in his songs. To write the lyrics, the Kerrs were joined by Joan Ford, a Colorado-born writer who was working on her first Broadway show. Anderson was kept busy throughout the production, constantly revising and rescoring the music. According to actress Pat Stanley, Anderson had little to do with the actual production of the show, by reason of either deferring to the more experienced Kerrs, or because his passive temperament was not suited for the often tempestuous nature of rehearsing and directing a Broadway show. He attended the rehearsals, but mostly was a ghostly presence, hovering and occasionally making discreet comments to producer Robert Whitehead or to the Kerrs.

Lunt-Fontanne Theatre
PLAYBILL
a weekly magazine for theatregoers
GOLDILOCKS

© Photofest

Playbill, October 1958, showing the opulent Egyptian set.

There were high expectations when *Goldilocks* made its debut on Broadway on October 11, 1958. There had been a lull in the Broadway season that year, with no new plays premiered for a six-month period; however, part of the reason for this was because of the durability of two smash hits, *West Side Story* and *The Music Man*, both of which were entering their second hugely successful years. In addition, Rodgers and Hammerstein's newest show, *Flower Drum Song*, would be making its debut in early December, and New York was thus in the midst of one of its most competitive seasons to date.

Critical reaction to *Goldilocks* was mixed. Despite the Kerrs' uproarious script, the stellar choreography of Agnes deMille, and Peter Larkin's elaborate and ornate Egyptian sets, it was the unconvincing love story between the two lead characters that caused audiences to reject the show. In a 2006 interview, co-stars Russell Nype and Pat Stanley reasoned that audiences were unable to get emotionally involved in the Ameche/Stritch relationship. Due to the adversarial on-stage antics between Ameche and Stritch's characters, *Goldilocks* was more a "Bickersons on Broadway" rather than a rival to *West Side Story's* heartbreaking Romeo and Juliet parable (Ameche and actress Frances Langford were famous for their sketches as the battling domestic couple, John and Blanche Bickerson, on radio).

Nype and Stanley also cited the deceptive title of the show itself that caused confusion and contributed to the show's early demise. *Goldilocks* had virtually nothing to do with the familiar fairy tale, other than a scene where Stritch dances with a bear, and both Nype and Stanley were convinced that if the show were called something else, it might have survived longer. Both agreed that "Lazy Moon," the title of the show-within-a-show, and also the name of the opening number, would have been a far superior title than *Goldilocks*.

Another problem with the show may have stemmed from the fact that the elaborate sets, most notably the Egyptian scene that was the setting for the movie being filmed by Don Ameche's character, was drawing attention from the story, the acting, and especially the songs. Russell Nype recalled a disgruntled George Abbott, the distinguished Broadway producer, muttering after the seeing the show, "People are going to leave the theater whistling the sets."

As a result of all of these aspects, *Goldilocks* survived a mere 161 performances, closing on February 28, 1959, after losing most of its 360 thousand dollar investment. Despite the financial failure of the show, supporting performers Russell Nype and Pat Stanley received Tony Awards, while nominations went to deMille, costume designer Antonio Castillo, and musical director Lehman Engel.

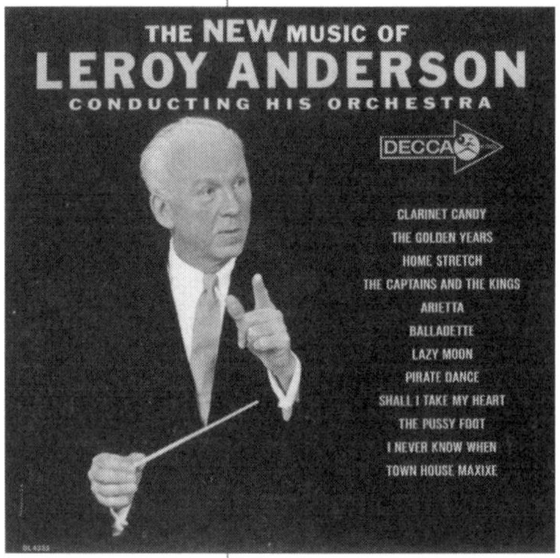
THE NEW MUSIC OF
LEROY ANDERSON
CONDUCTING HIS ORCHESTRA
DECCA
CLARINET CANDY
THE GOLDEN YEARS
HOME STRETCH
THE CAPTAINS AND THE KINGS
ARIETTA
BALLADETTE
LAZY MOON
PIRATE DANCE
SHALL I TAKE MY HEART
THE PUSSY FOOT
I NEVER KNOW WHEN
TOWN HOUSE MAXIXE

Decca LP, 1962, featuring instrumental versions of 6 songs from *Goldilocks*.

Following the closing of the show, Leroy Anderson rescored the music, not only to provide improvements, but also to make it adaptable for presentation by smaller companies and orchestras. In 1959, Anderson recorded stereo versions of many of his classic instrumental miniatures, including "Blue Tango," "Sleigh Ride," and "The Waltzing Cat." These were issued on the LP Leroy Anderson Conducts Leroy Anderson (Decca DL-8865), a record that also included two songs from Goldilocks, "Lady in Waiting" and "Pyramid Dance (Heart of Stone)." Six other songs from the show were recorded by Anderson on his 1962 LP, The New Music of Leroy Anderson (Decca DL-4335). In addition to the original Broadway cast album, which has since been reissued on CD by Sony Broadway, several of the songs from *Goldilocks* have been covered in vocal versions by singers including Karen Akers, Judy Kaye, Eileen Rodgers, and Vic Damone. Printed editions of the vocal versions have been unavailable for many years. Seven of the songs were originally published by Ankerford Music Corp. in a 1959 collection that is long out of print. In commemorating the 100th anniversary of the birth of Leroy Anderson, all songs from *Goldilocks* are being published in this collection for the very first time.

The Songs from *Goldilocks*

Despite the financial failure of *Goldilocks*, Leroy Anderson's score has gained increased attention and respect in the ensuing years. Although some of the songs are difficult to separate from the context of the show itself, others stand on their own as marvelous and delightful pieces of music. Probably the two most endearing of the lot are "I Never Know When" and "Lady in Waiting."

"I Never Know When (To Say When)" is an old-fashioned torch song, with Elaine Stritch's character, Maggie, coming to grips with the fact that she is not in love with millionaire George Randolph Brown (Russell Nype) and should stop leading him on. The song has a world-weary quality, the perfect saloon song for either a male or a female singer.

"Lady in Waiting" is one of Anderson's most charming melodies, resembling the best of Lerner and Loewe's graceful waltzes used in their own shows. Like many songs in Broadway shows, "Lady in Waiting" went through a series of changes before its lyrics were finalized. Although Anderson's melody remained unchanged, the title was originally called "London," containing lyrics that may have indicated a previous incarnation of the script. These lyrics were recorded as a demo by singer Patricia Wilson, who performed them for potential backers and stars, including actress Mary Martin. The original version retained the charm of the finalized version, but represented a completely different element of Pat Stanley's character, Lois Lee, a young ingénue who is attracted to Max Grady, the would-be movie mogul. Here are some of the original lyrics:

I've heard the bells of London town,
Silver bells, singing in Brooklyn,
That London Bridge was falling down,
Come to London, to London in spring.

But when I came to London town,
Somber bells seemed to be saying,
"Go home, go home," they seem to frown,
"Why be lonely in London in spring?"

Of the 23 songs from *Goldilocks* included in this collection, only 15 were utilized in the original production. The remaining eight songs were cut either in pre-production or during the out-of-town tryouts. These deleted songs are being presented in this collection for the first time along with the songs from the originally staged musical. Some of these songs, such as "Tagalong Kid," were performed by Nype and Stanley's characters, which were removed as their characters' roles were reduced, much to the actors' chagrin. It is likely that the songs that were cut had little or nothing to do with the quality of the songs themselves, but were dragged into oblivion in the process of the constant manipulation of the plot. In "Guess Who," Maggie (Stritch) sings a declarative love song in which nobody is more surprised than she to be in love *("I'm so cyclonic, you could bottle me for tonic. I'm frankly histrionic and frankly, I don't care, don't care, don't care!")* Max's comic song "Little Girls Should Be Seen," decrying the institute of marriage, includes the line, *"As you're leaving the church you are busting with pride, you don't know the minute you made her your bride, your darling Miss Jekyll became Missis Hyde...Little girls should be seen and not wed."*

Later Years

After the demise of *Goldilocks,* Leroy Anderson made one more attempt at a Broadway show, working on a musical version of Margaret Mitchell's epic *Gone With the Wind*, which was tentatively titled *Scarlett O'Hara*. He completed three songs for the score, collaborating on two with poet and lyricist Ogden Nash. One of these songs, "This Lovely World," had all the makings of an Anderson classic: a simple but eloquent melody, tender and evocative lyrics, and a beautifully bittersweet arrangement. This song has been included in this collection for the first time. *Scarlett O'Hara,* however, was never produced; the project was canceled before it could ever get off the ground.

Thanks to royalties from "Sleigh Ride" and his other works, Leroy Anderson spent the rest of his life comfortably, living with his wife Eleanor in the hilltop home he had built in Woodbury, Connecticut. In his last years, Anderson spent Friday nights at home playing cello in a string quartet he organized with friends.

Anderson (far right) enjoying his regular Friday evening of string quartet music, c. 1960s.

He continued to grant interviews and occasionally conduct his works, not discriminating between major orchestras such as the Hollywood Bowl Orchestra and smaller groups at schools and colleges. Several of these performances were released on record. One shining example

Rehearsing at Indiana State University, 1969.

was Anderson as a guest conductor with the Indiana State University Symphony Orchestra on May 14, 1969, an event that was recorded and released on the Century record label. In this program, the orchestra's leader, Dr. Earle Melendy, conducted the rarely heard "Alma Mater Scenes," which Anderson wrote in 1954.

In 1972, a special television broadcast of *Evening at the Pops* paid tribute to Anderson and his work. Maestro Arthur Fiedler invited Anderson to comment on his songs and even conduct several numbers. The loving accolades he received from the audience resulted in Anderson commenting later that the event was "the most important evening of my life." Leroy Anderson died of lung cancer on May 18, 1975, at the age of 66.

"An Evening at the Pops," PBS broadcast tribute to Anderson's music, July 4, 1972. L-R: Anderson and Arthur Fiedler.

The Leroy Anderson Legacy

This collection of music from Leroy Anderson's career is the first devoted solely to vocal editions of his music. Despite his reputation as a composer of light classical instrumentals, Anderson was responsible for a variety of songs with lyrics, thanks to his association with Mitchell Parish and the *Goldilocks* musical show. Still, with the exception of "Sleigh Ride," most people are unfamiliar with any vocal versions of his songs. To show evidence of a rarely seen side of his talents, we have also included two previously unpublished songs Anderson wrote in 1935, when he was about to embark on his association with Fiedler and the Boston Pops. These two songs, "The Music in My Heart" and "What's the Use of Love?" show that not only were Anderson's melodic talents fully developed at the age of 27, but he was also equally adept at writing meaningful, evocative lyrics.

In the three decades since his passing, Leroy Anderson's status as a composer has not diminished. At a 1973 lecture at Yale University, Anderson spoke of two prevailing myths: one was that enduring composers were never admired in their own lifetime; the other was that only so-called "serious" music would survive. In the case of Leroy Anderson, time is proving these myths to be false. Although he is chiefly known for only a handful of works, with many of them labeled as mere "novelties," Leroy Anderson's influence on other musicians and the memories of his fans, both old and new, are pronounced and incontrovertible. In honor of the centennial of his birth, Anderson's estate is publishing all of his orchestral and band music, making them available for schools and other institutions. Works such as "Sleigh Ride" and "The Syncopated Clock" have continued to be popular with these organizations, but now his entire oeuvre will continue to be available as well.

As for Anderson's current status, high praise has been extended from a variety of his peers. The late author and music historian Nicolas Slonimsky stated, "I think he was one of the most completely inventive composers who ever lived."

From John Williams: "His music remains forever as young and fresh as the very first day on which it was composed." In 1988, Anderson was posthumously inducted into the Songwriters Hall of Fame. In 1995, Harvard University named its band quarters the Anderson Band Center. A ballet, based on various Anderson works, was premiered by the San Francisco Ballet in 1999, and in 2003, the city of Cambridge, Massachusetts, dedicated a square to Anderson on the street across from the house where he grew up. At the dedication, which was attended by John Williams and current Boston Pops conductor Keith Lockhart, the Harvard Band played Anderson's music. As the centennial of his birth is celebrated, we hope that this collection of his vocal works will contribute to Anderson's thriving legacy.

LEROY ANDERSON

Anderson's star on the Hollywood Walk of Fame, located at 1620 Vine Street, near the former site of the Brown Derby Restaurant.

Anderson at home in 1971.

"I can't praise enough the work of Cary Ginell in putting together this excellent first-ever Leroy Anderson song folio."

—Eleanor Anderson (Mrs. Leroy Anderson)

Leroy Anderson

THE LEROY ANDERSON SONGBOOK · A CENTENNIAL CELEBRATION

Contents

BELLE OF THE BALL

Words by
MITCHELL PARISH

Music by
LEROY ANDERSON

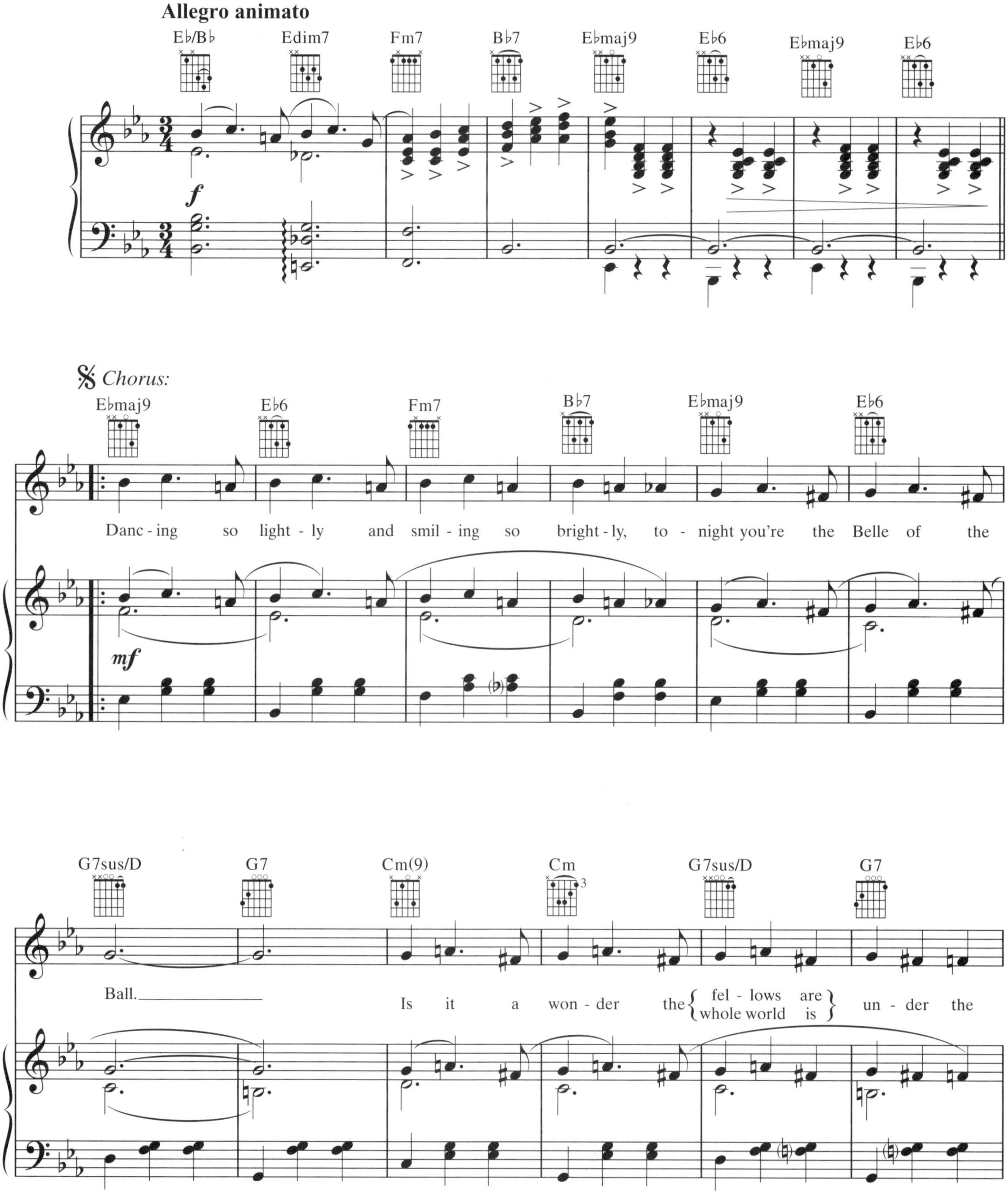
Allegro animato
Eb/Bb Edim7 Fm7 Bb7 Ebmaj9 Eb6 Ebmaj9 Eb6
f
Chorus:
Ebmaj9 Eb6 Fm7 Bb7 Ebmaj9 Eb6
Danc - ing so light - ly and smil - ing so bright - ly, to - night you're the Belle of the
mf
G7sus/D G7 Cm(9) Cm G7sus/D G7
Ball.
Is it a won - der the fel - lows are / whole world is un - der the

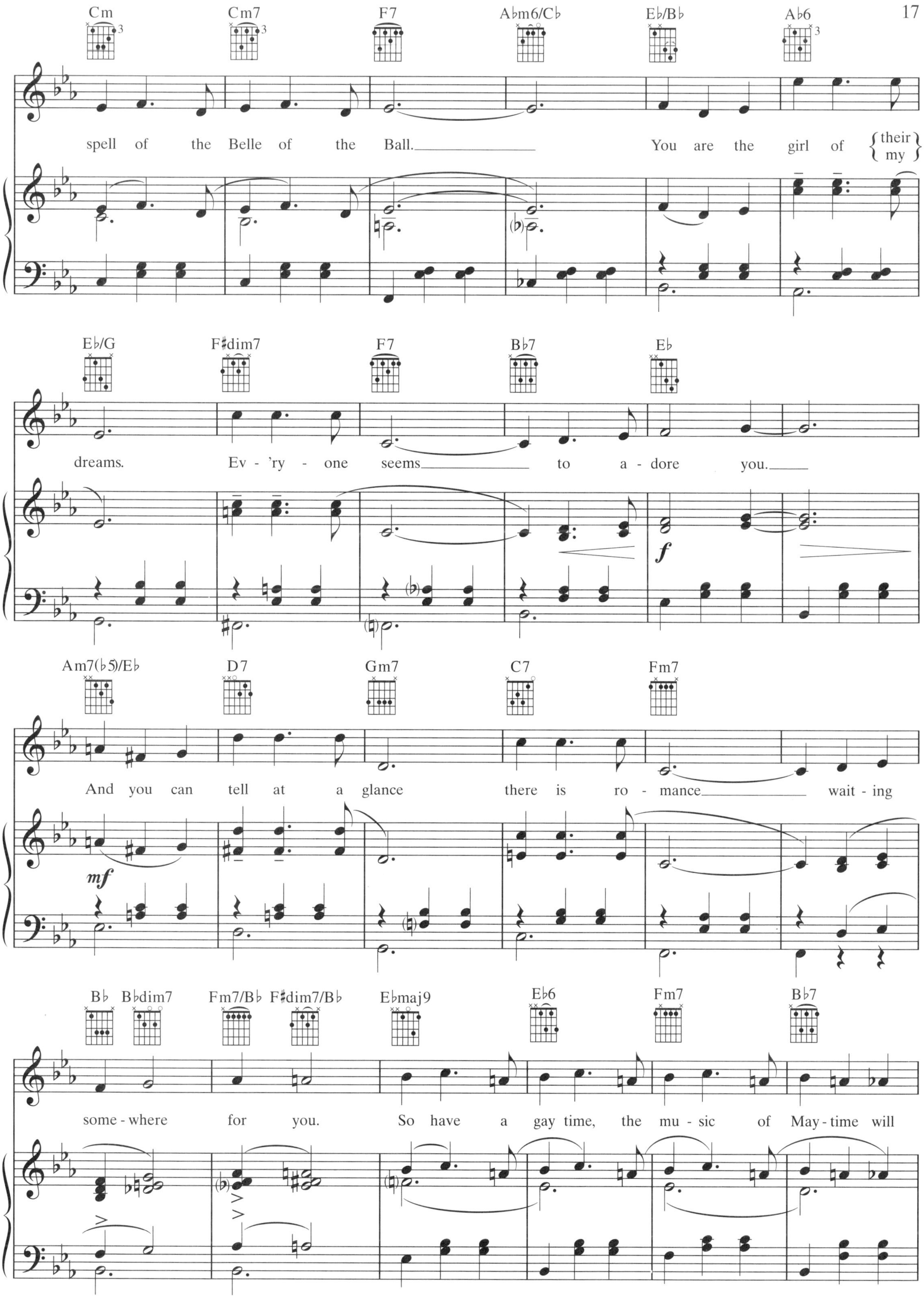
Cm Cm7 F7 A♭m6/C♭ E♭/B♭ A♭6
spell of the Belle of the Ball. You are the girl of {their / my}
E♭/G F♯dim7 F7 B♭7 E♭
dreams. Ev - 'ry - one seems to a - dore you.
Am7(♭5)/E♭ D7 Gm7 C7 Fm7
And you can tell at a glance there is ro - mance wait - ing
mf
B♭ B♭dim7 Fm7/B♭ F♯dim7/B♭ E♭maj9 E♭6 Fm7 B♭7
some - where for you. So have a gay time, the mu - sic of May - time will

E♭maj9 E♭6 G7sus/D G7 Cm(9) Cm
end with the break of the dawn. You and your laugh-ter will
G7sus/D G7 Cm Cm7 F7 A♭m6/C♭
lin-ger long af-ter the sound of the mu-sic is gone.
E♭/B♭ Adim7 A♭m6 E♭/G Cm F7
{We / I} will re-mem-ber the night. You were the fair-est of all.
poco rit.
D7/A E♭/B♭ E♭dim7 Fm7 B♭7
{In our hearts / In my heart} you'll be danc-ing for-ev-er and ev-er the Belle of the
a tempo
cresc.
rit.

1. E♭
Adim7/B♭
B♭7
2. E♭
Am7(♭5)
Ball.
f a tempo
Ball.
f a tempo
D
To Interlude
3.
E♭
Fm/E♭
E♭
Fine
To - Ball.
mp
f a tempo
ff
Interlude:
Am7
D7
Gmaj7
G6
Am7
D7
night there is mu - sic and danc - ing. The danc - ers are hap - py and
mp
Gmaj7
G7
C
Cm
G/B
B♭dim7
gay. To - night is a night for ro - manc - ing all the

Am7 D7 G Am7 D7
mag - i - cal hours a - way. And here in the crowd there is
Gmaj7 G6 Am7 D7 Gmaj7 G7
some - one with beau - ty as fresh as the dew. And
C Cm7 G/B B♭dim7 D/A Am7 C♯/A
you are that beau - ti - ful some - one, for the mo - ment you en - tered all
cresc.
D/A Am7 A7 D D7/C B♭7
D.S. 𝄋 al Fine
glanc - es were cen - tered on you.
f

BLUE TANGO

Words by
MITCHELL PARISH

Music by
LEROY ANDERSON

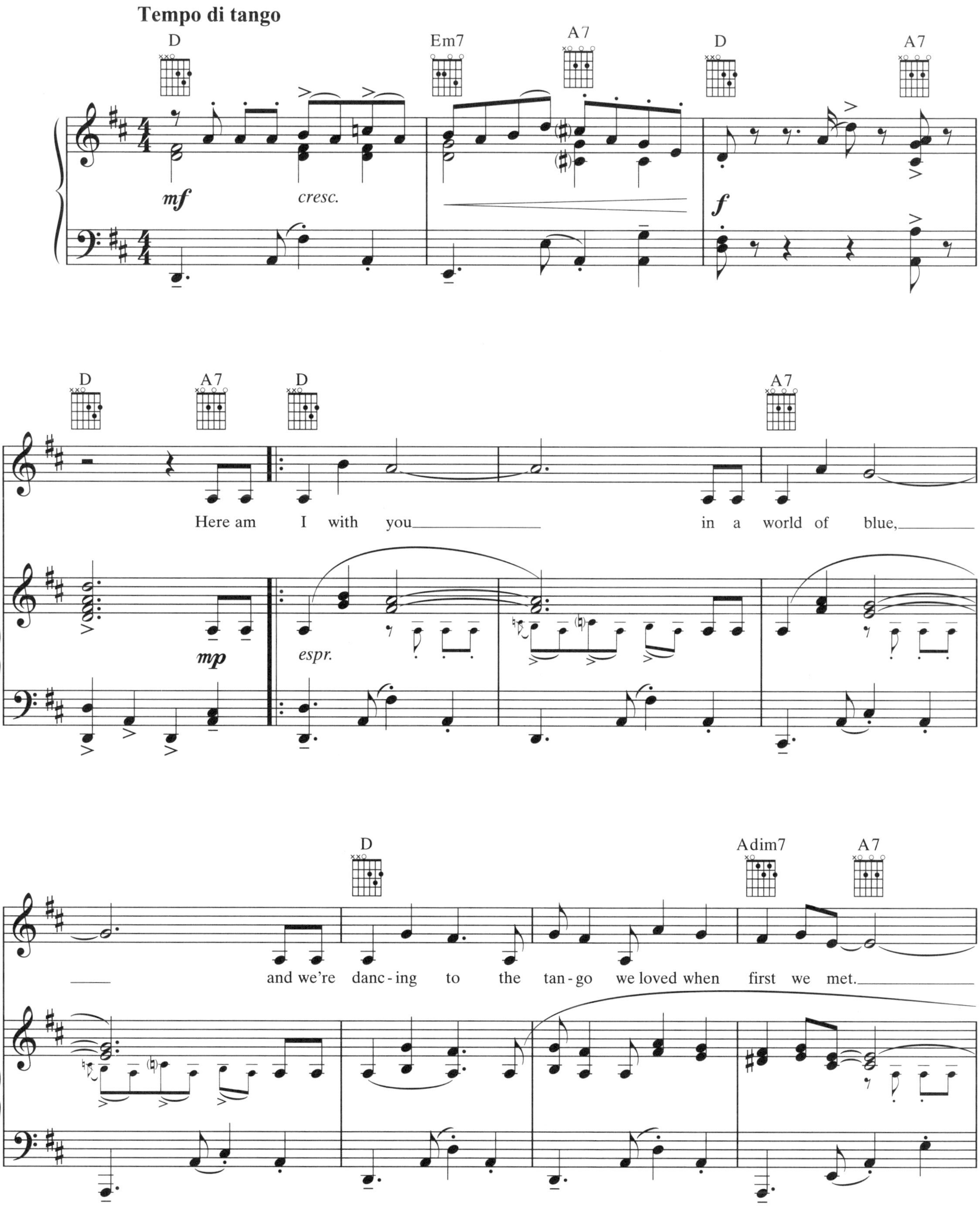
Tempo di tango
D
Em7
A7
D
A7
mf
cresc.
f
D
A7
D
A7
Here am I with you in a world of blue,
mp
espr.
D
Adim7
A7
and we're danc-ing to the tan-go we loved when first we met.

D
A7
While the mu - sic plays, we re - call the days
D
A7
D
when our love was a tune that we could - n't soon for - get.
D7
G
D
As I kiss your cheek, we don't have to speak.
mf
A7
Em7
Adim7
A7
D
The vi - o - lins, like a choir, ex - press the de - sire we used to know not long a -

D7 G D
go. So just hold me tight in your arms to - night,
mp
A7 Em7
1.
Adim7 A7 D
and this blue tan-go will be our thrill-ing mem-o-ry of love.
mf
cresc.
Em7 A7 D A7 D A7
Here am
f
mp
2. Adim7 A7 D D6
thrill-ing mem-o-ry of love.
f

FORGOTTEN DREAMS

Words by
MITCHELL PARISH

Music by
LEROY ANDERSON

Medium Tempo
Voice
Piano
mf
rall.
mp
a tempo
D
Em7
A7
They keep re - turn - ing,
F♯m7
D
D7
G
Gm6
through years of yearn - ing: No mat - ter how you try, For-
got - ten dreams won't die.
You think it's o - ver,
p
for - ev - er o - ver, And then a voice will sigh: "For -

D A7 D Bm E7 C#m7 F#m7
got - ten dreams won't die." Some - where, in a crowd-ed place,
Bm7 E7 A Gm7 C7 Am Bm7
Though she is-n't there you will see her face; Some - where, you will hear her name, And
(he) (his) (his)
A Adim E7 A Em7 A7
sud-den-ly you know that the thrill is still the same. (You're still re-
p(echo)
Em7 A7 D Em7 A7
mem-ber-ing the thrill.) One day you loved her,
(him)
mf
mp
p

F♯m7 D D7 G Gm6
one day you lost her, (him) And now you won - der why For-
Ped. Ped. *
D A7 D Em7 A7
got - ten tears won't dry. They keep re - turn - ing,
p mp
F♯m7 D D7
the flame still burn - ing: Though love has
Ped.
G Gm6 D A7 D
rall.
said good - bye, For - got - ten dreams won't die.
rall. p pp
Ped. * Ped.

SERENATA

Words by
MITCHELL PARISH

Music by
LEROY ANDERSON

Beguine tempo
Fm/C
C7(♭9)
Fm/C
f
Verse:
Fm
C7sus
C7(♭9)
Love - ly song of love, the mu - sic
p
Fm
C7sus
C7(♭9)
Gm7(♭5)
of a sil - ver star; won't you be my ser - e -
colla voce
rit.
sfz

C C7/B♭ A♭ C7
nade that's soft - ly played on my gui - tar? To -
mp
a tempo
Chorus:
F F♯dim7 Gm7 Gm7/C C7
night, while all the world is still, here I
mp
Fmaj7 Dm9 G7 G13 Bdim7
stand un - der her win - dow - sill. Sing to my
F/C Gm7 C7 Fmaj7 F6 Em7 A9
loved one, Ser - e - na - ta, for me. Sing her your

Dmaj9
D6
Adim7/G
Gm7
Gm7(♭5)/B♭
Gm7(♭5)
C7(♭9)
song, love's mel - o - dy. So
mf
F
F♯dim7
Gm7
Gm7/C
C6
C7(♭9)
near, yet we're so far a - part, here I'll
Fmaj7
Dm9
G7
G13
Bdim7
stand till I have won your heart. Go to my
F/C
Gm7
C9
Am7(♭5)/E♭
C/D
D9
loved one, Ser - e - na - ta, and say, "When you're in
f
rit.

F/G G7 D♭6/C C7(♭9)
1. F6 Gm7 C7
love, love finds a way.” To -
dim.
mp a tempo
mf mp
2. F6 Gm7 Fm Gm7(♭5) Cm7
way.” Love al - ways finds a
a tempo
Fm Gm7 C7 F Gm7 C7
way. I'll win her heart some -
F E♭m6 F E♭m6 F
day.
dim. al fine
p

SLEIGH RIDE

Words by
MITCHELL PARISH

Music by
LEROY ANDERSON

Moderately bright
D7 Gmaj7 G6 Gmaj9 G6
mf
Just hear those
Gmaj7 G6 Am7 D7 Gmaj7 G6 Am7 D7
sleigh bells jin - gle - ing, ring - ting - tin - gle - ing too. Come on, it's
Gmaj7 G6 Am7 D7 G B♭ D7
love - ly weath - er for a sleigh ride to - geth - er with you. Out - side the

Gmaj7 G6 Am7 D7 Gmaj7 G6 Am7 D7
snow is fall - ing and friends are call - ing, "Yoo hoo." Come on, it's
Gmaj7 G6 Am7 D7 G C G C G
love - ly weath - er for a sleigh ride to - geth - er with you. Gid - dy -
C♯m7 F♯7 B
yap, gid - dy - yap, gid - dy - yap, let's go, let's look at the show,
C♯m7 F♯7 B F♯ B F♯ B
we're rid - ing in a won - der - land of snow. Gid - dy -

Bm7 E7 A
yap, gid - dy - yap, gid - dy - yap, it's grand, just hold - ing your hand.
Am7 D7 Am7/D D7
We're glid - ing a - long with a song of a win - ter - y fair - y - land. Our cheeks are
Gmaj7 G6 Am7 D7 Gmaj7 G6 Am7 D7
nice and ros - y and com - fy co - zy are we. We're snug - gled
Gmaj7 G6 Am7 D7 G B♭ D7
up to - geth - er like two birds of a feath - er would be. Let's take that

Gmaj7 G6 Am7 D7 Gmaj7 G6 Am7 D7
road be - fore us and sing a cho - rus or two. Come on, it's
Gmaj7 G6 Am7 D7
1. To Interlude
G C G C G D7
love - ly weath - er for a sleigh ride to - geth - er with you. There's a
2. Fine
Gmaj7 G6 Gmaj7 G6 Gmaj7 G
you.
dim.
p
f
Interlude:
Gmaj7
birth - day par - ty at the home of Farm - er Gray, it - 'll

G6
be the per - fect end - ing of a per - fect day. We'll be
G♯dim7 Am7 A♯dim7 G/B B7 Em C♯m7(♭5)
sing - ing the songs we love to sing with - out a sin - gle stop, at the
legato
B/F♯ C♯m7(♭5) C♯m7 F♯7 B G♯dim7 D7
fire - place while we watch the chest - nuts pop. Pop! Pop! Pop! There's a
Gmaj7
hap - py feel - ing noth - ing in the world can buy, when they

pass a - round the cof - fee and the pump - kin
G6 G♯dim7 Am7 A♯dim7
pie. It - 'll near - ly be like a pic - ture print by
legato
G/B B7 Em A7 D C/D
Cur - ri - er and Ives. These won - der - ful
D C/D D C/D D C/D D7
D.S. 𝄋 al Fine
things are the things we re - mem - ber all through our lives! Just hear those

THE SYNCOPATED CLOCK

Words by
MITCHELL PARISH

Music by
LEROY ANDERSON

Moderately
A7
D
A7
(Clock imitation)
There was a man like you and me,_ as
(Clock imitation cont.)
mf
D
A7
D
A7
sim - ple as a man could ev - er be, and he was hap - py as a king,_ ex -
G6
B7/F♯
D♯dim7
Em
B♭7(♯5)
A7
D
A7
D
A7
cept for one pe - cu - liar thing. He had a clock that worked all right;_ it

D A7 D A7
worked all right, but not ex - act - ly quite. In - stead of go - ing "Tick, tock, tick," the
G6 B7/F♯ D♯dim7 Em B♭7(♯5) A7 D D7 G G♯dim7 Dmaj7/A Fdim7
cra - zy clock went "Tock, tick, tock." The poor old man just raved and raved, be -
Em7 A9 F♯m7(♭5) B7 Em F♯7 A♯dim7 Bm
cause no - bod - y could say why his sil - ly clock be - haved that
E7 B♭6 A7 D A7
hick - o - ry dick - o - ry way. But now a fa - mous man is he; he

D A7 D
owns a pub - lic cu - ri - os - i - ty. From far and wide the
A7 G6 B7/F♯ D♯dim7 Em B♭7(♯5) A7 D
peo - ple flock to hear the syn - co - pat - ed clock.
D7 C/D D D7(♭9) Em7/D D7(♭9) Em7/D G♯dim7 Am D7
cresc.
f
Tick - a -
Gmaj7 G6 Am7(4) D7 Am7(4) D7
tock, tick - a - tock; there's a zing in the swing of that

Gmaj7 G6 F♯m7(4) B Em9 Em Em7(4) A7
clock. Tock-a - tick, tock-a - tick; don't you think it's a mar-vel-ous
D7sus D Gmaj7 G6 Am7(4) D7 Am7(4) D7
trick? Ting-a - ling, ting-a - ling; there's a zong in the bong of that
Gmaj7 G6 F♯m7(4) B Em9 Em Em7(♭5)
ring. Ling-a - ting, ling-a - ting; don't you think it's a won-der-ful
A7 D A7
thing? The ex - perts came to hear and see, but
mf

D A7 D A7
none of them could solve the mys - ter - y. They called Pro - fes - sor Ein - stein, too; he
G6 B7/F♯ D♯dim7 Em B♭7(♯5) A7 D A7 D A7
said, "There's noth - ing I can do." But soon the fick - le hu - man race will
D A7 D A7
find an - oth - er freak to take its place, and one fine day the man will hock the
G6 B7/F♯ D♯dim7 Em B♭7(♯5) A7 D N.C. A7 D
poor old syn - co - pat - ed clock.

THE WALTZING CAT

Words by
MITCHELL PARISH

Music by
LEROY ANDERSON

Moderate waltz tempo
8va
mf
l.h.
VERSE
Bbm7 Bbdim Abmaj7 Ab6 Bbm7
There once was a tom-cat, a won-der-ful tom-cat, who had all the
mf
Eb7 Bbm7 Eb7 Abmaj7 Ab6 Bbm7 C7
u - su - al faults, But this cat was diff - 'rent, what
Fm Abm Eb Bb7 Eb
made him so diff - 'rent was his in - cli - na - tion to waltz,

slower
Eb dim
Eb7
Each night this fe-line Sir to his la-dy fair would purr:
CHORUS
Moderate waltz tempo
Ab Db6 Cm Ab6 Ab Bbm
I love to waltz (me - ow) On a night like
mf
Gb Eb7 Ebdim Eb7 Ab Db6 Cm Fm
this with stars in the skies, Come, let us waltz (me - ow)
Abm Eb Ebdim Fm7 Bb7 Eb
While I look in - to your love-ly green eyes. I

A little brighter.
D♭ B♭m A♭
nev-er knew what a lit-tle waltz can do, Till the night I
E♮dim Fm B♭7 Ddim
danc'd with you, Light-ly as a feath-er, let's pus-sy-foot to-geth-er,
molto rall.
A♭ B♭m7 Cm E♭m6 F7 F+ F7 B♭m Cdim B♭m7
I'd love to spend (me - ow) all my nine lives just
a tempo
rit.
D♭m A♭6 E♭7 A♭ E♭7 A♭
waltz-ing with you. you.
a tempo
f

SLEIGH RIDE
CHILDREN'S EDITION
THE SYNCOPATED CLOCK
CHILDREN'S EDITION
THE WALTZING CAT

Leroy Anderson at home in 1950 with his son Eric and daughter Jane.

Above are children's editions of three of his most popular collaborations with lyricist Mitchell Parish.

VOCAL SELECTION
THE PRODUCERS THEATRE presents
A ROBERT WHITEHEAD PRODUCTION
DON AMECHE ELAINE STRITCH
In The New Musical
GOLDILOCKS
with
RUSSELL NYPE PAT STANLEY
NATHANIEL FREY MARGARET HAMILTON
Book by WALTER and JEAN KERR
Music by LEROY ANDERSON
Lyrics by WALTER and JEAN KERR and JOAN FORD
Dances and Musical Numbers staged by AGNES DE MILLE
Directed by WALTER KERR
Settings by PETER LARKIN
Costumes by CASTILLO
Lighting by FEDER
Musical Director LEHMAN ENGEL
Orchestrations by LEROY ANDERSON and PHILIP J. LANG
Dance Music Arranged by LAURENCE ROSENTHAL
ANKERFORD MUSIC CORP.
SOLE SELLING AGENT
MILLS MUSIC, Inc.
1619 BROADWAY, NEW YORK 19, N. Y.
PRICE
$2.00

Cover of original "Goldilocks" song folio, 1958.

From the Musical Production "GOLDILOCKS"

BAD COMPANIONS

Words by
JOAN FORD, JEAN KERR
and WALTER KERR

Music by
LEROY ANDERSON

Andante maestoso

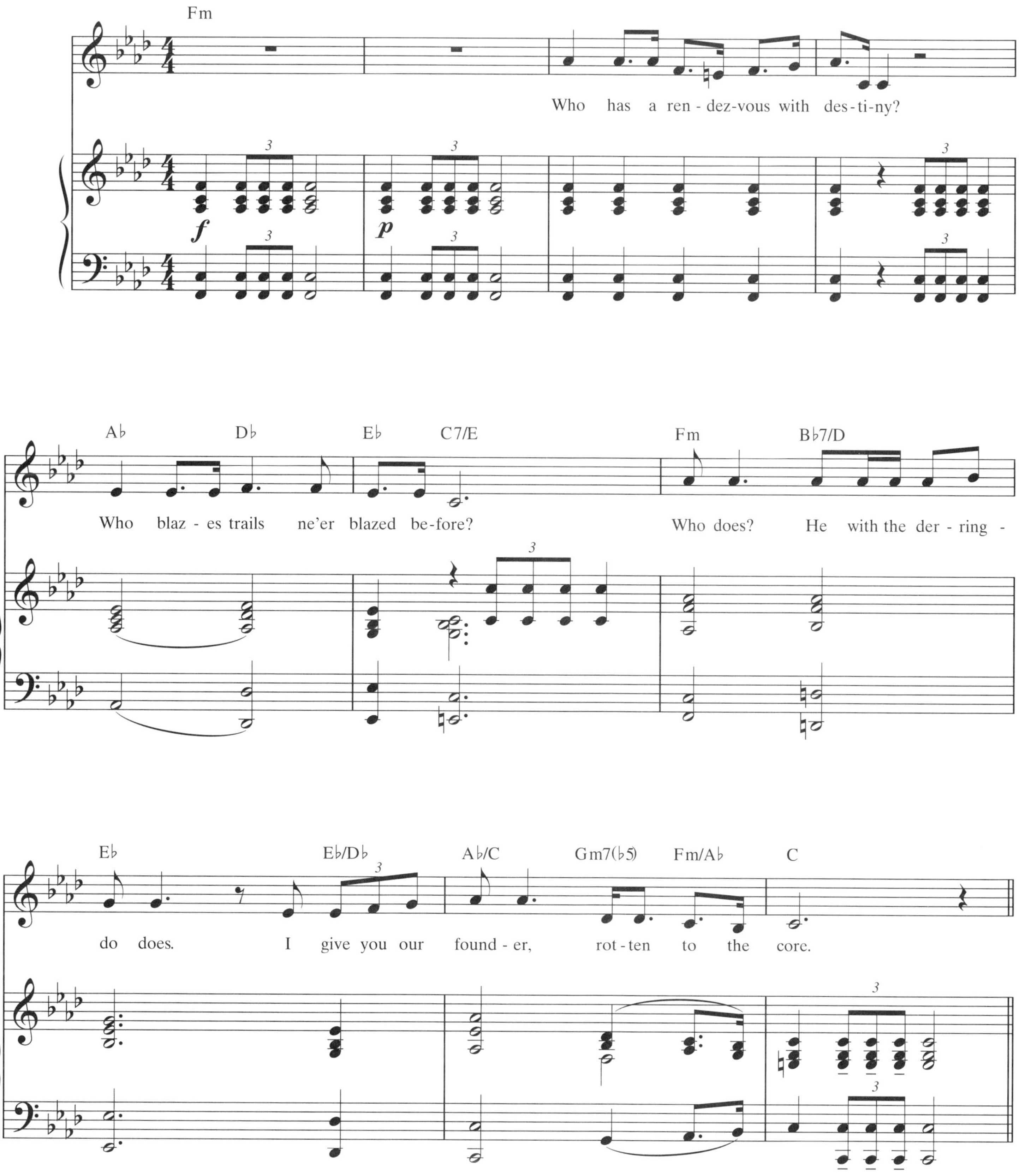
Fm
Who has a ren - dez-vous with des-ti-ny?
A♭ D♭ E♭ C7/E
Who blaz - es trails ne'er blazed be-fore?
Fm B♭7/D
Who does? He with the der - ring -
E♭ E♭/D♭ A♭/C Gm7(♭5) Fm/A♭ C
do does. I give you our found - er, rot - ten to the core.

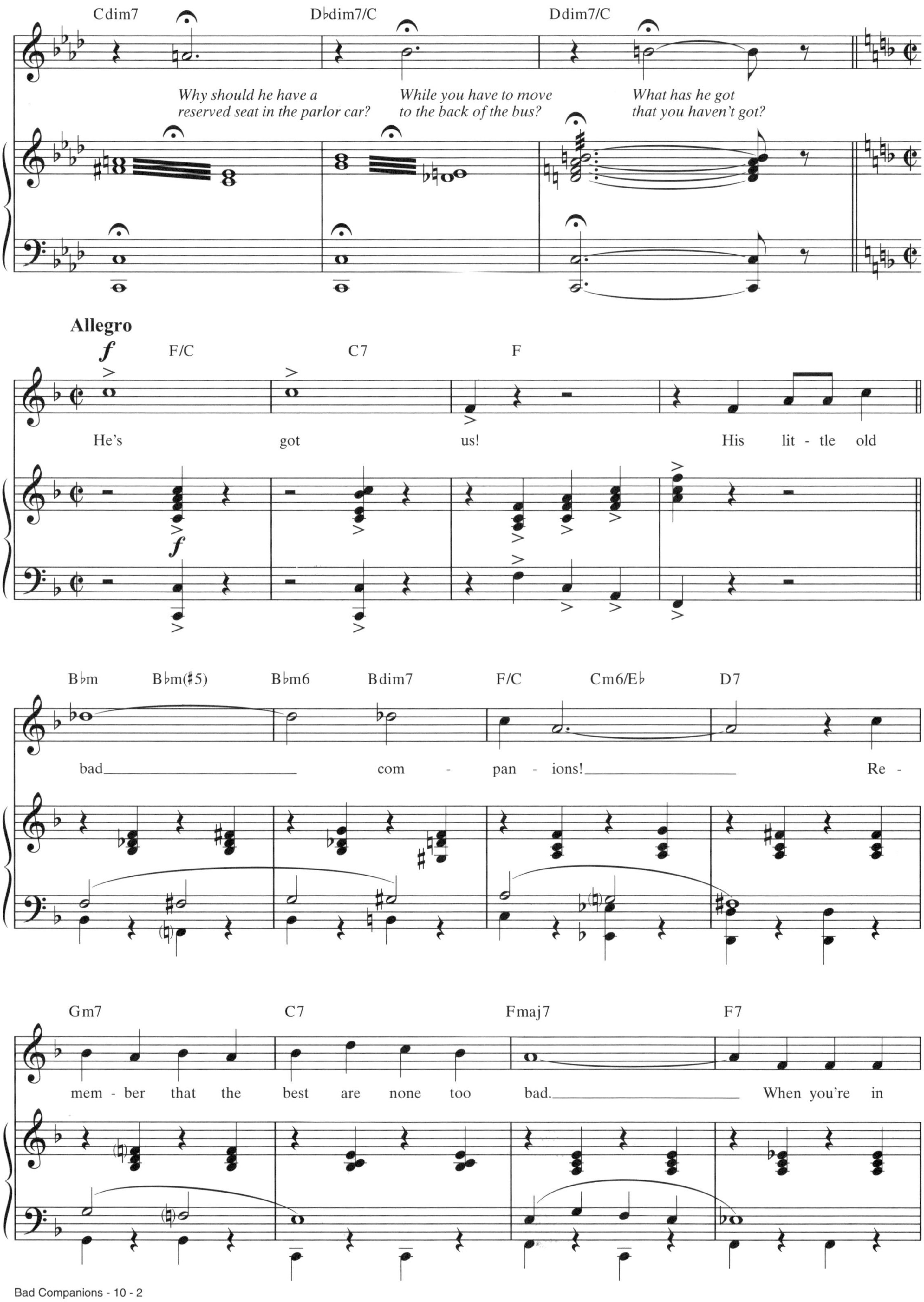
Cdim7
D♭dim7/C
Ddim7/C
Why should he have a reserved seat in the parlor car?
While you have to move to the back of the bus?
What has he got that you haven't got?
Allegro
f
F/C
C7
F
He's got us! His lit - tle old
B♭m
B♭m(♯5)
B♭m6
Bdim7
F/C
Cm6/E♭
D7
bad com - pan - ions! Re -
Gm7
C7
Fmaj7
F7
mem - ber that the best are none too bad. When you're in

B♭6
Bdim7
F/C
F/E♭
B♭6/D
B♭m/D♭
jail, there is no doubt you need a pal to help you out, you need your
F/C
F♯dim7
C7
F
A♭
C7/G
bad, bad, bad com - pan - ions.
f
F
A♭
C7/G
F6
It's known that Jes - se James could shoot, but
p
did you know he drank? And who held good old Jes - se up while

B♭m B♭m(♯5) B♭m6 Bdim7
he held up the bank? It was his bad com -
F/C Cm6/E♭ D7 Gm7 C7
pan - ions! Re - mem - ber that the best are none too
Fmaj7 F7 B♭6 Bdim7
bad. When you swear off wine and song, you need a
F/C F/E♭ B♭6/D B♭m6/D F/C F♯dim7 C7
friend to set you wrong, you need your bad, bad, bad com -

F Ab C7/G Gb A Db7/Ab
pan - ions.
f
Gb6
Gen - ghis Khan was sat - is - fied to give his foes a trim - min'. Who
p
did the drea - ry rou - tine work of rav - ish - ing the wom - en? His lit - tle old
Cbm Cbm(#5) Cbm6 Cdim7 Gb/Db Dbm/Fb Eb7
bad com - pan - ions! Re -

A♭m7 D♭7 G♭maj7 G♭7
mem - ber that the best are none too bad.________ When your
C♭6 Cdim7 G♭/D♭ G♭/F♭ C♭6/E♭ C♭m6/D
wife runs off with a brand - new mate, you need a friend to cel - e - brate, you
G♭/D♭ Gdim7 D♭7 G♭ A D♭7/A♭
need your bad com - pan - ions.
G B♭ D7/A G6
His moth - er called him Per - ci - val when

he was but a nip - per. Who broke him of his sis - sy ways and
Cm Cm(♯5) Cm6 C♯dim7
made him Jack The Rip-per? It was his bad com -
G/D Dm6/F E7 Am7 D7
pan - ions! Re - mem - ber that the best are none too
Gmaj7 G7 C6 C♯dim7
bad. When you've in - sured your la - dy love, you need a

G/D G/F C6/E Cm6/E♭ G/D G♯dim7 D7
help - ing hand to shove, you need your bad, bad, bad com -
G B♭ D7/A A♭ C♭ E♭/B♭
pan - ions.
A♭5
Ag - o - wak the Can - ni - bal king ate those whom he de - feat - ed. Who
Toms
went and got bi - car - bon - ate when - ev - er they re - peat - ed? His lit - tle old

D♭m
A♭/E♭
bad ___ com - pan - ions.
Adagio
D♭m
Ddim7 A♭/E♭ E♭m6/G♭ F
(Spoken:) A good bad companion is lazy, shiftless, yellow, treacherous, corrupt, dirty, insubordinate, and always there when you need him.
Bad ___ com - pan - ions, ___ re -
p
B♭m
A♭
A♭7
mem - ber that the best are none too
bad.
are none too bad.
When mu -
Tempo I
D♭6
Ddim7
A♭
A♭7
se - ums made of wax im - mor - tal - ize our gra - cious Max, let no one

D♭6 Ddim7 A♭ A♭7
min - i - mize his fame, he plays a dirt - y, filth - y game. But it takes
D♭6 Ddim7 A♭ D♭6/F D♭m6/F♭
more than grit like his to be the son - of - a - b that he is, it takes his
(grit and spunk to be a first rate no good skunk, it takes your)
A♭/E♭ A♭+/E♭ D♭/E♭ E♭7
bad, bad, bad com -
A♭
pan - ions!
ff

From the Musical Production "GOLDILOCKS"

THE BEAST IN YOU

Words by
JOAN FORD, JEAN KERR
and WALTER KERR

Music by
LEROY ANDERSON

Allegro vivace
G/D
D7
G/D
To the na - ked eye, you're ab - so - lute - ly peer - less, you're
f
mp
simile
D7
G/D
Am/D
G/D
D
C/D
D
G
G♭+
E♭m6/G♭
Gm/F
brawn - y, brain - y, fear - less, and you know what you're a - bout. And I tell my - self no
F7
B♭/F
F7
B♭/F
F
E♭/F
F
mat - ter what a mess I'm in, you're such a man - ly spec - i - men, you'll sure - ly get me
Andante
B♭
E♭6
F/E♭
B♭/D
B♭
B♭/D
3
out. But would you? Or have I mis - un - der - stood you? When I'm in a

C♭/E♭ F/E♭ B♭/D B♭ Gm Dm/F N.C. Dm/F N.C.
cri - sis and ask what your ad - vice is, do you know how you'd an - swer?
Allegro vivo
Em7(♭5) N.C. D D/C Em7(♭5)/B♭ D/A D D/C Em7(♭5)/B♭ D/A
Do you know what you'd do?
1. The
sfz
f
Gm Gm(maj7) Gm7 C9
scene is dark - est Af - ri - ca, the wa - ter's nice and hot, the
(2.) pair of sav - age blood-hounds are a - thirst - ing for the kill. If
mp
B♭/F B♭maj7 B♭7 B♭6 B♭7
can - ni - bals have got me salt - and - pep - pered for the pot. But
one should fail to eat me up, the oth - er sure - ly will. They're
cresc.

Dm
Dm(maj7)
Dm7
you come run - ning to the fray, and this is what you
gain - ing fast with o - pen jaws, you en - ter and we
Bm7(♭5)
Cm7
say: "But, dearest, cannibals have rights just like other people."
pause: "Darling, what did you do to provoke those dogs?"
That's what you'd
Cm7/F
B♭
E♭
Cm7(♭5)
do, that's ex - act - ly what you'd do. Where is the beast
f
D7(♭9)
1.
Gm
2.
Maestoso
Gm7
in you? 2. A you?
f

G♭+
B♭/F
F7
I don't ask for a high - mind - ed
B♭/F
Dm/F
E♭/F
F7
B♭
he - ro, as fair and un - der - stand - ing as can be,
A7
Dm
A7
Dm
Gm7
al - ways read - y to pur - sue the oth - er fel - low's point of view, al - ways
F/C
C7
F
E♭
Cm7
search - ing for the truth to make us free. He's a lib - er - al? Well,

Più lento
F Eb Dm Cm7 F/C Am7(b5) D Eb/D
dan - dy! It's just that I de - mand he be a nar - row - mind - ed, small - ho - ri - zoned,
p
E/D Dm7 Gb/D Ddim7 D7
par - ti - san, o - pin - ion - at - ed, big - ot - ed, re - ac - tion - ar - y mule when it comes to
colla parte
Tempo I
D D/C Em7(b5)/Bb D/A D D/C Em7(b5)/Bb D/A Gm Gm(maj7)
me. I'm hud - dled on the door - step and I
Gm7 C9 Bb/F Bbmaj7 Bb7
can - not pay the rent, the land - lord with the mus - tache is an e - vil, leer - ing

B♭6 B♭7 Dm Dm(maj7) Dm7
gent. But through the blind - ing snow you come to tell your lit - tle
Bm7(♭5)
chum: "Tenants never do understand these things. It costs money to run an apartment."
Cm7 Cm7/F B♭ E♭ B♭/D
That's what you'd do, that's ex - act - ly what you'd do. Where, oh where is the
Cm7(♭5) F7(♭9) B♭
beast in you?
f

From the Musical Production "GOLDILOCKS"

(Give the Little Lady)

A GREAT BIG HAND

Words by
JOAN FORD, JEAN KERR
and WALTER KERR

Music by
LEROY ANDERSON

Vivo
Am7/D
Dm7/G
G7
mf
Cmaj9
F/C
Cmaj9
No tears___ for me, boys.___ I'll tell ya what I'm go - ing to
D7
C6/G
A13
A7(♯5) A9
be, boys.___ The per - fect la - dy, the way I planned._ So,
Dm7
G7
Cmaj9
give the lit - tle la - dy a great big hand.___ Rag - time,___ you're

F/C Cmaj9 D7
through now. No hon-ky-tonk pi - an - o will do now. It's
C6/G A13 A7(♯5) A9 Dm7
Bach for me on the ba - by grand. So, give the lit-tle la-dy a
Dm9 G13(♭9) C6 E♭7 A♭ A♭+ E♭9 A♭+
great big hand. I'm through pre - tend - ing this
Gm7(♭5) C7 Gm7 C7 Fm
in - ge - nue has found her hap - py

A♭7
A♭9
G13
end - ing. The trunk I was born in is at - tic bound. So,
Cmaj9
F/C
Cmaj9
you take the gay time, for me, it's gon - na be P. T.
D7
C6/G
A13
A7(♯5) A9
To Coda
A. time. I found the way to the prom - ised land. So,
Dm7
Dm9
G9
G13(♭9)
C6
give the lit - tle la - dy a great big won - der - ful hand. Good -

Dm7 Dm7/G G9 Cmaj9 Dm7 Dm7/G G9
bye, good - bye to the day coach, to the grease paint and the
Cmaj9 Fm7 B♭7 E♭maj7
two - a - day. There's been a switch in the play, coach. When the
Am7(♭5) A♭7 G Dm7(♭5)
whis - tle starts a - blow-in', the la - dy is go - in' a - way. Fare - well!
G Dm7(♭5) G Dm7(♭5) G7 D.S. 𝄋 al Coda
Fare - well! I'm gon-na miss you more than I can tell. Go!
sfz

Coda
Dm7
E♭dim7
C/E
give the lit - tle la - dy…
ya know I wan - na be a
E♭dim7
Dm7
la - dy!
So, give the lit - tle la - dy a
Dm9
G13
G13(♭9)
C6
great big won - der - ful hand!
D♭9(♯11)
C

From the Musical Production "GOLDILOCKS"

HEART OF STONE

(Pyramid Dance)

Words by
JOAN FORD, JEAN KERR
and WALTER KERR

Music by
LEROY ANDERSON

Allegro vivace
mf
C Eb Db C Eb Db Bb C Eb Db C
Love - ly HEART OF STONE, you prom - ised par - a -
mp
Gm7 C9 F Ab Gb Eb F Ab Gb Eb F Ab Gb Eb
dise; How could I have known you told a
F Ab G7 C Eb Db Bb C Eb Db Bb C Eb
thou - sand love - ly lies? Oth - er

D♭ C E♭ D♭ B♭ C E♭ D♭ C Gm7 C9
loves than mine will flame and fade a - way,
F A♭ G♭ E♭ F A♭ G♭ E♭ F A♭ G♭ E♭ F A♭
Ash - es at your shrine, poor dust - y loves of
G♭ C E♭ D♭ B♭ C E♭ D♭ B♭
yes - ter - day.
(Duet)
Gm7 C7 C+ E♭7 A♭
HEART OF STONE, you
C7-9 Fm Gm7 F♯dim. C7 C+ E♭7 A♭ C7-9 F A♭ G♭ E♭
are a dev - il with a face as fair as morn -

a2
F Ab Gb Eb F Ab Gb Eb F F7 Bbm F Dm7 G7 G+
ing. Give your
Bb Eb B dim. B+ Dm7 C7-9 B dim. B+ Bb7 Eb B dim. a2 C Eb
heart a - way for on the des - ert wind I hear a warn -
Db Bb C Eb Db Bb C Eb Db Bb C Eb Db C
- ing.
R.H.
Gm7 C7 C+ Eb7 Ab C7-9 Fm Gm7 F# dim. C7 C+ Eb Ab C7-9
Time will find you where this bright pa - vil - ion stands and leave no

a2
F Ab Gb Eb F Ab Gb Eb F Ab Gb Eb F F7
to - - ken.
Bm F Dm7 G7 G+ Bb Eb B dim. B+ Dm7 C7-9 B dim. B+
Just a leg - end and up - on the sigh - ing
Bb7 Eb B dim. C Db Gb maj. 7
sum - mer sands a bro - - ken HEART
G7 C Eb Db Bb C Eb Db Bb C
OF STONE.
R.H.

From the Musical Production "GOLDILOCKS"

I CAN'T BE IN LOVE

Words by
JOAN FORD, JEAN KERR
and WALTER KERR

Music by
LEROY ANDERSON

Allegro agitato
G
Dm7/G G Dm7/G G
I can't be in love, I
can't be in love, I
G7 Dm7/G
can't be in love. You can see that I'm
can't be in love. For the rec - ord I'm
C(9) N.C. Am7(♭5)
(a) un - sta - ble, (b)
(a) neu - rot - ic, (b)
mp
f
N.C. G/D N.C.
un - a - ble, (c) un - pre - pared to mar - ry her or an - y
quix - ot - ic, (c) id - i - ot - i - c'lly in-clined to cut - ting
A9
oth - er.
ca - pers.
G(9)/D G/D D7sus D7
It's an in - con - ve - nient time and fur - ther - more I'm much too young to leave my
I'm a ne'er-do - well and sure as hell I'd nev - er learn to share the morn - ing

G
Dm7/G
G
Dm7/G
moth-er.
pa-pers.
I can't be in love, I
I can't be in love, I
mp
f
G7
Dm7/G
C(9)
Am7(♭5)
can't be in love. It's ap - par - ent I'm (a) too risk - y, (b)
can't be in love. Mat - ri - mo - ny is (a) too stick - y, (b)
mp
N.C.
G/D
N.C.
A9
too frisk - y, (c) just a guy of un - re - li - a - ble li - bi - do.
too trick - y, (c) I be - lieve I'll leave the li - on's den to Dan - iel;
f
G(9)/D
G/D
D7sus
D7
I am sure to stray and an - y - way I sim - ply do not own a good tux -
an - y time that I got lone - ly I have on - ly got to get a cock - er
mp

G
B♭
F
e - do.
span-iel.
Yes,
she's
Str.
Br.
Am11
D7
Am11
D7
D7/G
Gm7
sweet,
yes,
she's
C9
Edim7
F6
B♭maj9
F6
B♭6
clev - er.
I
ad -
A7
Em7/A
A7
D7
Am7
G♯dim7
D7
mit I could sit and look in her eyes, her beau - ti - ful eyes for -
Br.

Bdim7 D7
N.C.
Dm7/G
G
Dm7/G
ev - er. Nev-er! I can't be in love,
I
mp
f
G7/D
Dm7/G
C(9) N.C.
Am7(♭5)
can't be in love.
For the rec - ord I'm (a) un - stead - y, (b)
Heav - en knows I've been 'round a - plen - ty, clowned
N.C.
G/D N.C.
A9
un - read - y, (c) un - a - vail - a - ble in cer - tain bus - y sea - sons;
a - plen - ty, found lov - er's lane a most en - chant - ing place to vis - it;
(f)
To Coda
G(9)/D
G/D
D7sus
D7
I am poor and im - ma - ture and un - em - ployed and then be - sides I have my
now I
mp

G G7 C G5 C G5 C G5 C G5
rea-sons. You
mf
f
C G5 C G5 C G5 C G5 C G5 C G5 C G5 C G5 C G5 C G5
see be - fore you a man who had his life all planned, who wan - dered down life's
mp
C G5 C G5 C B B7/D♯ Em F♯7 B F♯5 B F♯5 B F♯5 B F♯5
high - way hand in hand in hand in hand in hand in hand,
cresc.
f
B F♯5 B F♯5 B F♯5 B F♯5 B F♯5 B F♯7 B Emaj7
ask - ing lit - tle, tak - ing all, bru - nettes in sum - mer, blondes in

A E5 A E5 A G A E Em
meno mosso
fall. (Spoken:) Now look at me! Slain, slain, slain! By the near - est smile, the
mf
allarg.
f
p
Tempo I
Em(maj7) Em7 A9 G(9)/D G/D Gmaj7/D G6/D
mer - est smile, the dear - est smile that ev - er drove a
pp
mp
cresc.
D7sus/A D7 Am11 D7 G
D.S. 𝄋 al Coda
rov - ing man in - sane. I
f
𝄌 Coda
G(9)/D G/D Gmaj7/D G/D D7sus/A D7
want to plant my feet there, there's a girl I want to meet there that I would-n't dare to cheat there. If this
mp

Am11 D7 G
car - ing is - n't real - ly love, what is it? I
Dm7/G G/D Dm7 G Dm7/G G/D G
can't be in love, can't be in love, I
Dm7/G Dm7
can't be, can't be, can't. I can't be in
G N.C. G
love. Could I?
f
p
(f)
p
f
p
ff

From the Musical Production "GOLDILOCKS"

I NEVER KNOW WHEN
(To Say When)

Words by
JOAN FORD, JEAN KERR
and WALTER KERR

Music by
LEROY ANDERSON

Andante ritmico
Verse
I
Eb6
A(b5)
knew on the day I met him, He was-n't the man for me; I
Eb6
F7
Fm7
Bb7
knew I should just for - get him, But I had to stay and see.
rall.

Chorus

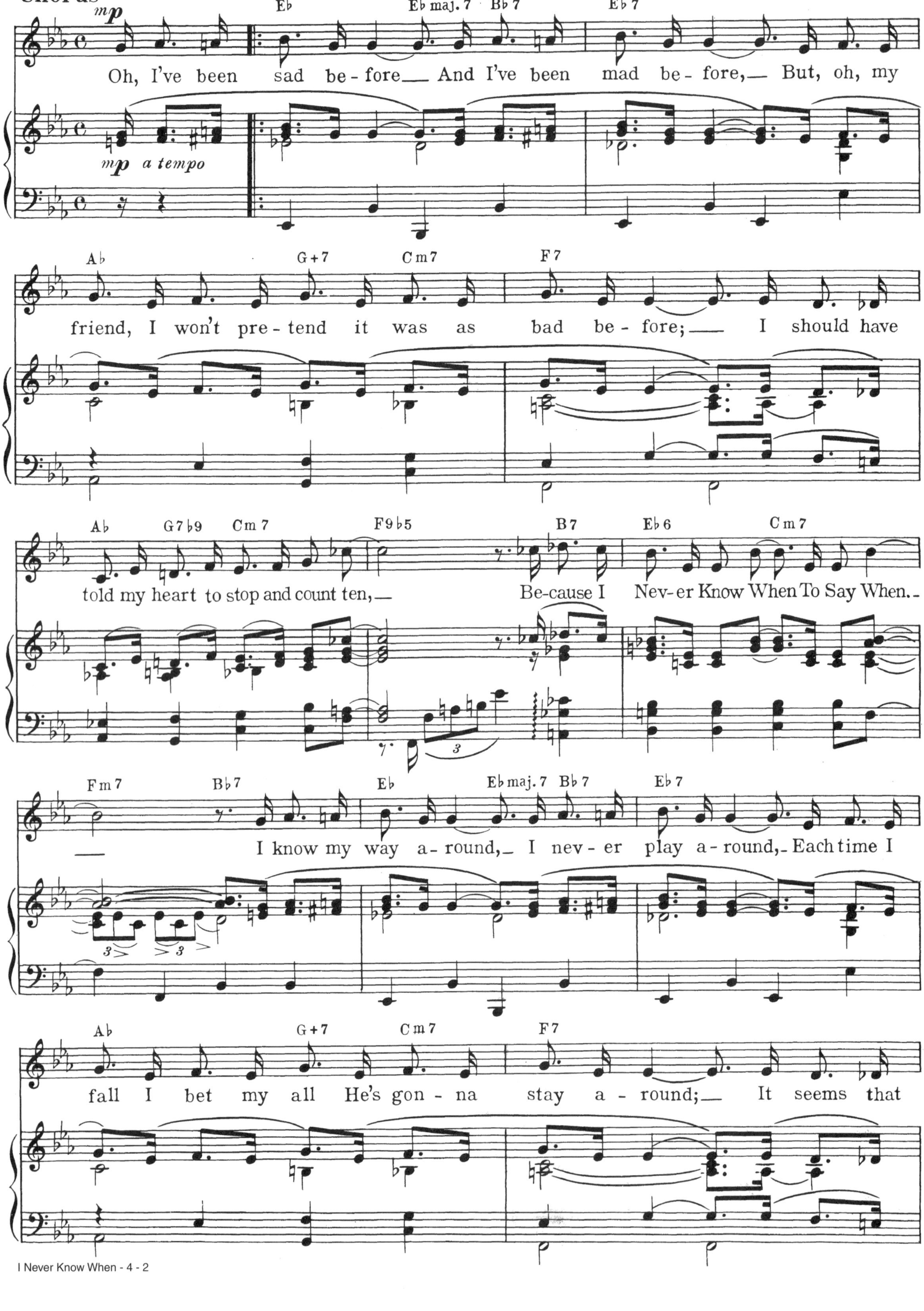
mp
Eb Eb maj. 7 Bb7 Eb7
Oh, I've been sad be-fore And I've been mad be-fore, But, oh, my
mp a tempo
Ab G+7 Cm7 F7
friend, I won't pre-tend it was as bad be-fore; I should have
Ab G7b9 Cm 7 F9b5 B7 Eb6 Cm7
told my heart to stop and count ten, Be-cause I Nev-er Know When To Say When.
Fm7 Bb7 Eb Eb maj. 7 Bb7 Eb7
I know my way a-round, I nev-er play a-round, Each time I
Ab G+7 Cm7 F7
fall I bet my all He's gon-na stay a-round; It seems that

A G7♭9 Cm7 F9♭5 B7 E♭6 Fm7
ev-'ry-thing is ros-y and then Some-how I Nev-er Know When To Say When.
E♭6 A B♭+7♭9 E♭maj.7 E♭6
But now I've learned my les-son, And it's an
Fm7 B♭7 E♭maj. 9 E♭6 Am7♭5 D7 D7♭9
eas - y one: You've got-ta keep them
Gm7 C7 Fm E dim. Fm7 B♭7
guess-'in', Keep it fun, kiss and run. The skies are
E♭ E♭maj.7 B♭7 E♭7 A♭ G+7 Cm7
storm-y now, My dreams all bore me now, No can-dle lights the lone-ly nights that lie be -

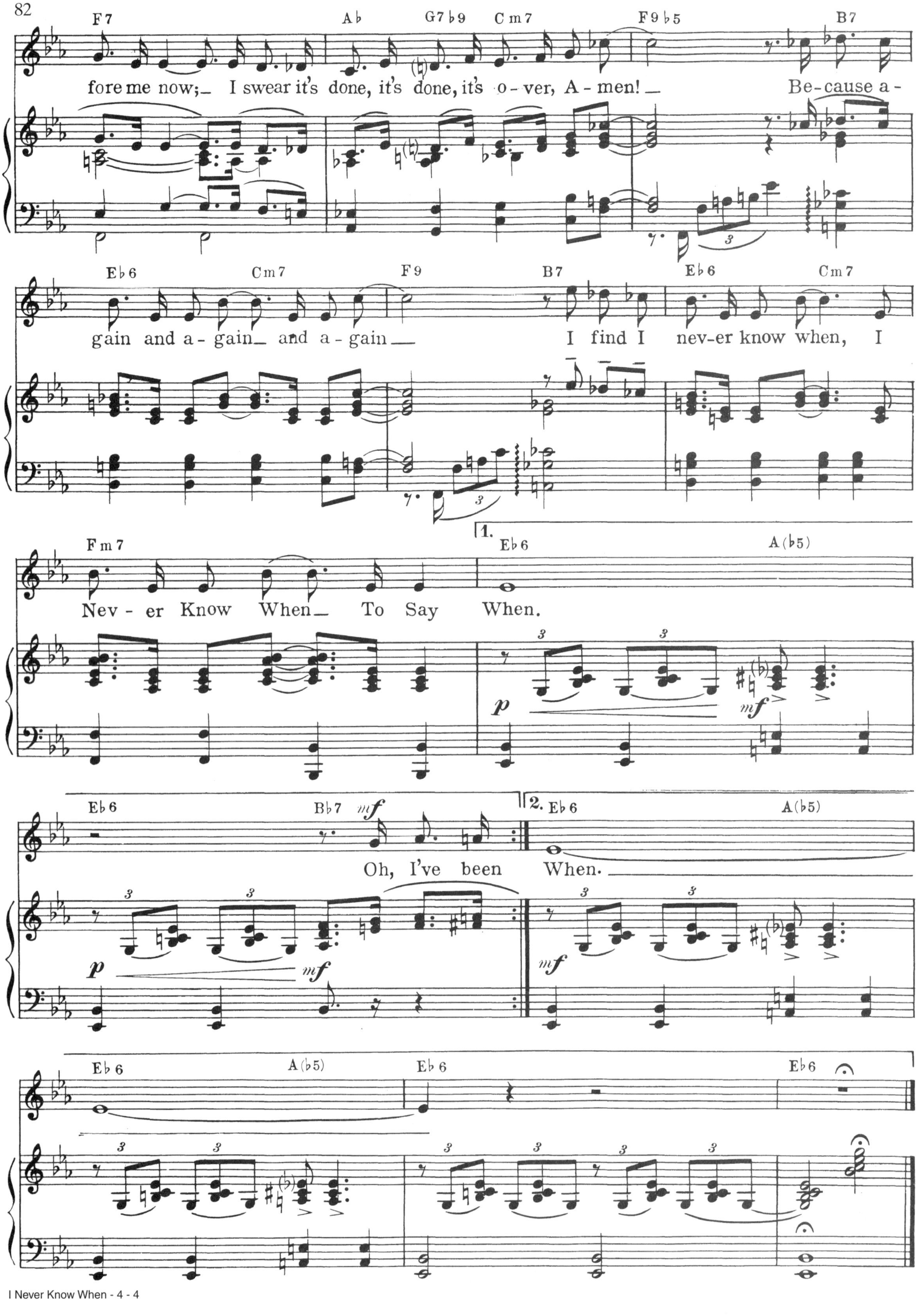
F7 Ab G7b9 Cm7 F9b5 B7
fore me now; I swear it's done, it's done, it's o-ver, A-men! Be-cause a-
Eb6 Cm7 F9 B7 Eb6 Cm7
gain and a-gain and a-gain I find I nev-er know when, I
Fm7
Nev-er Know When To Say
1.
Eb6 A(b5)
When.
p
mf
Eb6 Bb7
mf
Oh, I've been
p
mf
2.
Eb6 A(b5)
When.
mf
Eb6 A(b5) Eb6 Eb6

From the Musical Production "GOLDILOCKS"

LADY IN WAITING

Words by
JOAN FORD, JEAN KERR
and WALTER KERR

Music by
LEROY ANDERSON

Allegro moderato
f
Lois:
Eb Eb maj. 7 Eb7 Ab Fm7b5 Eb
1. When I've had much too much to dream, And I seem
lite hus - sars and brave dra - goons, Whole pla - toons
mf
F7 Bb7 Bb9 Bb7 Eb Eb maj. 7 Eb7
pleas - ant - ly tip - sy, Pre - tend - ers plot and princ - es
duel for my fa - vor, While pale com - pos - ers spin their
1. 2.
Ab Fm7b5 Eb Bb7 Eb6 Bb7 Fm7 Bb7 Eb Eb
scheme, All for love of a la - dy like me. 2. Po -
tunes, All for love of a la - dy like me.

Poco più mosso
F7(sus B♭)
F7
B♭maj. 7
B♭6
F7(sus B♭)
La - dy In Wait - ing, pa - tient - ly wait - ing, wait - ing for
mf
F7
B♭
F7(sus B♭)
F7
some - one to fetch and to car - ry me, Ev - er so light - ly,
B♭maj. 7
B♭6
F7(sus B♭)
F7
B♭
E dim.
hold - ing me tight - ly, In - to the night where he might e - ven
rall.
Fm7
B♭7
Lois:
E♭
E♭maj. 7
E♭7
A♭
mar - ry me. I chase the boys who make me cry,
mf a tempo

George:
Fm7♭5 E♭
Why, oh, why?
Lois:
F7 B♭7 B♭9 B♭7 E♭ E♭maj.7
Gen - u - ine gen - tle - men Seem to be in
E♭7 A♭ Fm7♭5
short sup - ply.
George:
E♭ B♭7 E♭6 B♭7 Fm7 B♭7 E♭
Stuff and non-sense and fid - dle - dee - dee!
Lois:
E♭6
I
Più mosso
Cm7 F7 B♭6 E♭ E♭ Fm7 B♭7 B♭7 E♭
wish I could turn back the al - ma - nac; I'd chase the gents and they'd chase me
wish I could make the di - rec - tions plain: You can't say "Tar zan" till he says
mf
E♭ Cm7 F7 E♭ F♯dim. F♮m7 Fm7♭5
1.
back. I'd go off my trol - ley for Sir Wal - ter Ra - leigh and Ra - leigh'd
"Jane." Let him play the sheik, you play hide and go seek, You have

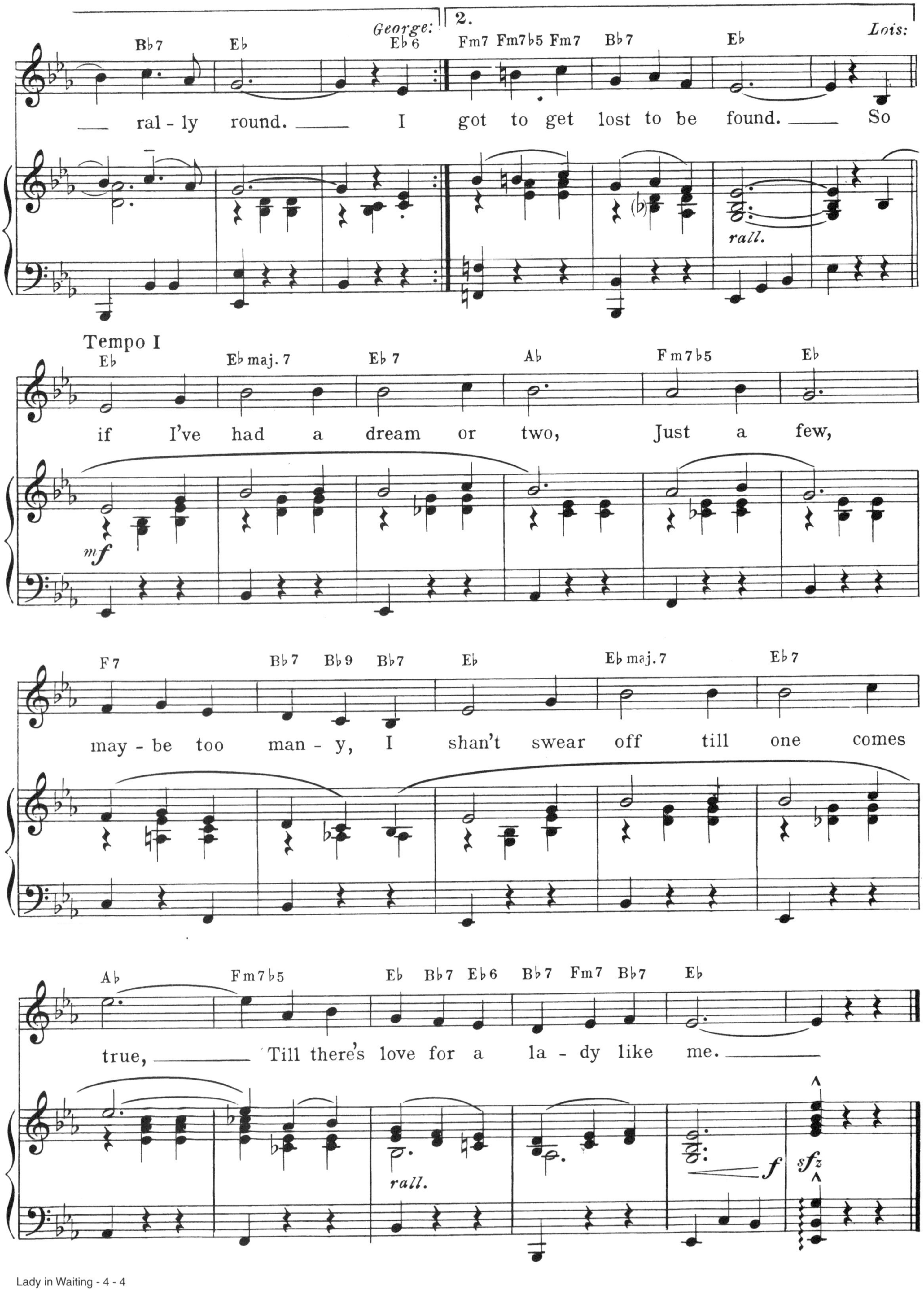
George:
2.
Lois:
Bb7 Eb Eb6 Fm7 Fm7b5 Fm7 Bb7 Eb
ral - ly round. I got to get lost to be found. So
rall.
Tempo I
Eb Eb maj. 7 Eb 7 Ab Fm7b5 Eb
if I've had a dream or two, Just a few,
mf
F7 Bb7 Bb9 Bb7 Eb Eb maj. 7 Eb7
may - be too man - y, I shan't swear off till one comes
Ab Fm7b5 Eb Bb7 Eb6 Bb7 Fm7 Bb7 Eb
true, Till there's love for a la - dy like me.
rall.
f
sfz

From the Musical Production "GOLDILOCKS"

LAZY MOON

Words by
JOAN FORD, JEAN KERR
and WALTER KERR

Music by
LEROY ANDERSON

Moderate fox-trot
mf
Verse
F Fmaj.7 F6 F Am7 Ab dim. C7
John-ny took his Jen-ny for a stroll in the park, One fine June night;
mp
Gm D+ Gm7 C7 C9(+5) F
Jen-ny looked at John-ny and she said, "It's so dark,— Where's the moon-light?"
Cm D7 Cm D7 Dm7 G7
John-ny liked the dark, 'cause he was feel-ing ro-man-tic, But Jen-ny would-n't spark and it was

Dm7 G7 G9 C7 Gm7 D#m6 C7
driv-ing him fran-tic, At last he raised his head up and cried:
Refrain
F Bb F C#dim. Dm G7 Dm7
Shame on you, moon, blame on you, moon,
Time to get up, you good - for - noth-ing LA - ZY
mp-mf
G7 C7 Gm7 C7
How can you be so persnick-et-y? Shame on you, moon, blame on you, moon, This lit-tle ro-mance is rick-et-y.
MOON, Up-sy-dai - sy moon, Need your
F Dm Gm7 C7 F
help to make my ba-by tell me "yes." in-stead of "may be." But be - fore she will kiss me,

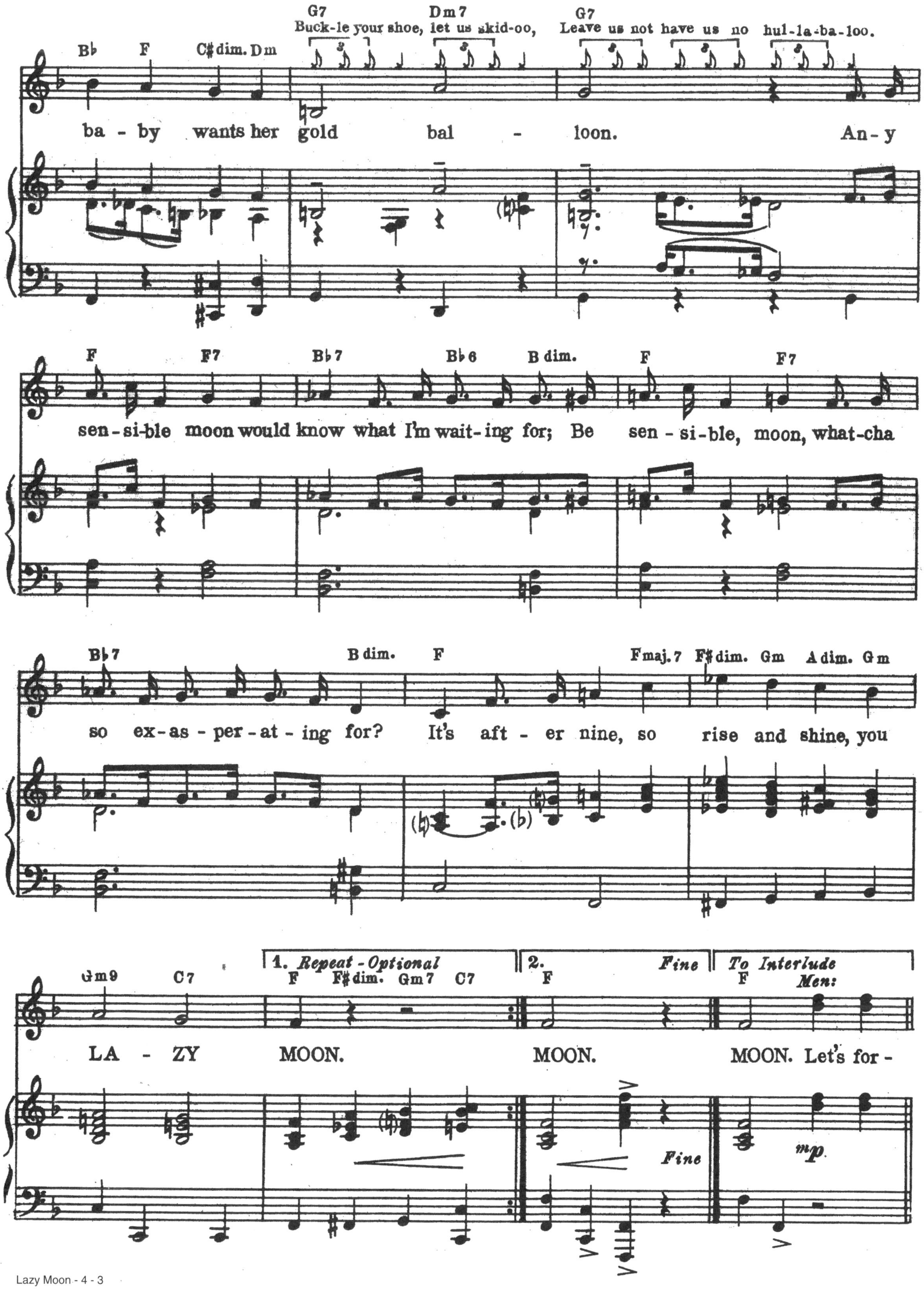
Buck-le your shoe, let us skid-oo, Leave us not have us no hul-la-ba-loo.
G7 Dm7 G7
Bb F C#dim. Dm
ba - by wants her gold bal - loon. An - y
F F7 Bb7 Bb6 B dim. F F7
sen-si-ble moon would know what I'm wait-ing for; Be sen - si-ble, moon, what-cha
Bb7 B dim. F Fmaj.7 F#dim. Gm A dim. Gm
so ex-as - per-at - ing for? It's aft - er nine, so rise and shine, you
1. Repeat - Optional
2.
Fine
To Interlude
Gm9 C7 F F#dim. Gm7 C7 F F
Men:
LA - ZY MOON. MOON. MOON. Let's for -
Fine
mp

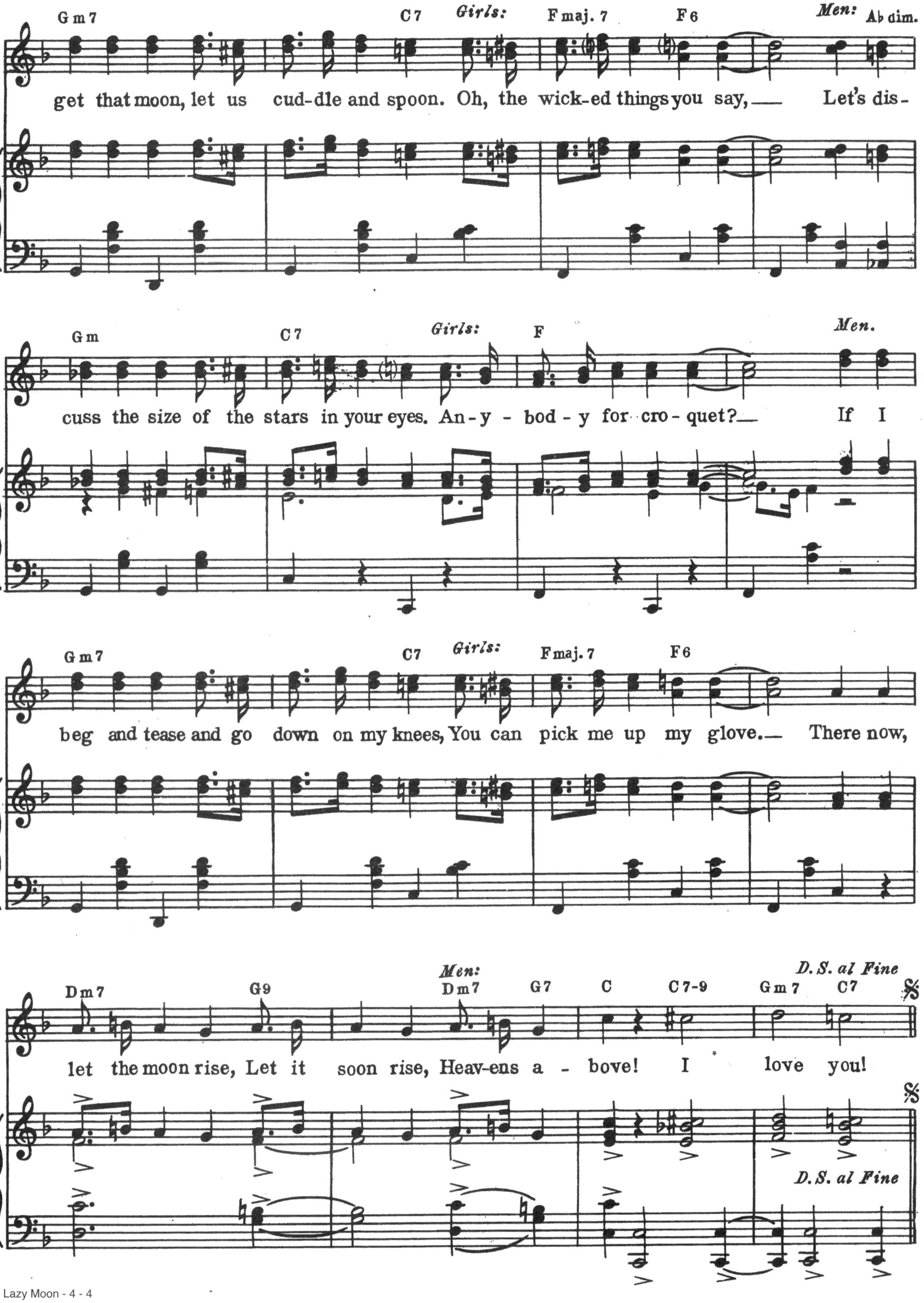
Gm7 C7 Girls: Fmaj. 7 F6 Men: A♭dim.
get that moon, let us cud-dle and spoon. Oh, the wick-ed things you say, Let's dis-
Gm C7 Girls: F Men.
cuss the size of the stars in your eyes. An-y-bod-y for cro-quet? If I
Gm7 C7 Girls: Fmaj. 7 F6
beg and tease and go down on my knees, You can pick me up my glove. There now,
Dm7 G9 Men: Dm7 G7 C C7-9 Gm7 C7
D. S. al Fine
let the moon rise, Let it soon rise, Heav-ens a-bove! I love you!
D. S. al Fine

From the Musical Production "GOLDILOCKS"

NO ONE WILL EVER LOVE YOU

Words by
JOAN FORD, JEAN KERR
and WALTER KERR

Music by
LEROY ANDERSON

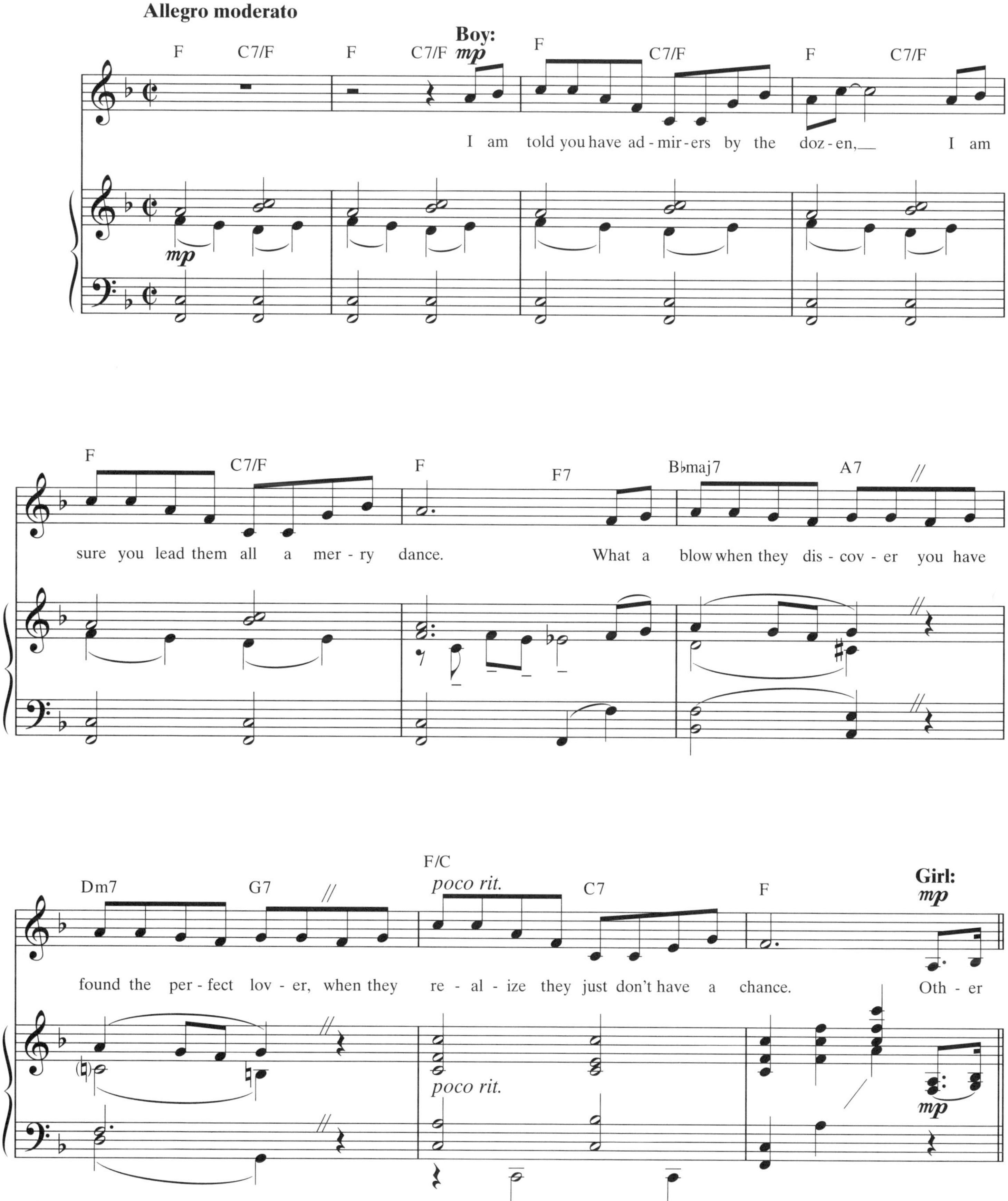
Allegro moderato
Boy:
mp
F C7/F F C7/F F C7/F F C7/F
I am told you have ad - mir - ers by the doz - en, I am
F C7/F F F7 B♭maj7 A7
sure you lead them all a mer - ry dance. What a blow when they dis - cov - er you have
Dm7 G7 F/C C7 F
poco rit.
Girl:
found the per - fect lov - er, when they re - al - ize they just don't have a chance. Oth - er

Refrain: with mock sweetness
F C7 Gm7 C7 Gm7 C7
hearts may flut - ter when they see you pass - ing by, oth - ers turn to but - ter ev - 'ry
F F7 B♭9 Bdim7
insultingly
f
time they hear you sigh. Me, I love the love-light in your bead - y lit - tle eye, but
F/C Dm7 Gm7 C7 F C7
Boy: sweetly
mp
no one - 'll ev - er love you like you do. Some go all to piec - es when they
Gm7 C7 Gm7 C7 F
see that girl - ish grin, some would write a the - sis on the tex - ture of your skin. I a-

F7 B♭9 Bdim7 F/C G7
insultingly
f
dore the dim-ple in that small re-ced-ing chin, but no one-'ll ev-er love you like
C7(♭9) F6 Cm F7 B♭
Girl: sweetly
mp
you do. I can see this is no ca-su-al af-fair;
Cm F7 B♭ Dm7 G7
Boy:
Girl:
when did you first be-gin to care? Were you child-hood sweet-hearts, did you
C(9) C6 G7 C♯dim7 G7 Gm7 G7(♭9) C7
Boy:
stand be-neath a tree with a heart carved on it and "I love me?" Might-y

F C7 Gm7 C7 Gm7 C7
ar - mies slum - ber with your pic - ture by their beds, an im - pos - ing num - ber kiss the
F F7 B♭9 Bdim7
Girl:
insultingly
Both:
ground your slip - per treads. Then there's me, I've saved a curl from both your lit - tle heads, but
F/C G7 Gm7 C9 F6
no one - 'll ev - er love you like you do.

From the Musical Production "GOLDILOCKS"

THE PUSSY FOOT

Words by
JOAN FORD, JEAN KERR
and WALTER KERR

Music by
LEROY ANDERSON

Bright ragtime tempo
mf
Verse
B♭7 E♭ F7 B♭7 E♭ F♯dim.
When I pick my puss-y foot up, Each lov-in' Tom a - long the
mp
B♭7 Fm7 B♭7 E♭ A♭ E♭ B♭7 E♭
fenc - es sens - es some-thin' new. When I put my puss-y foot
F7 B♭7 E♭ Cm D7
down, Each hap-py fe - line makes a bee - line to play

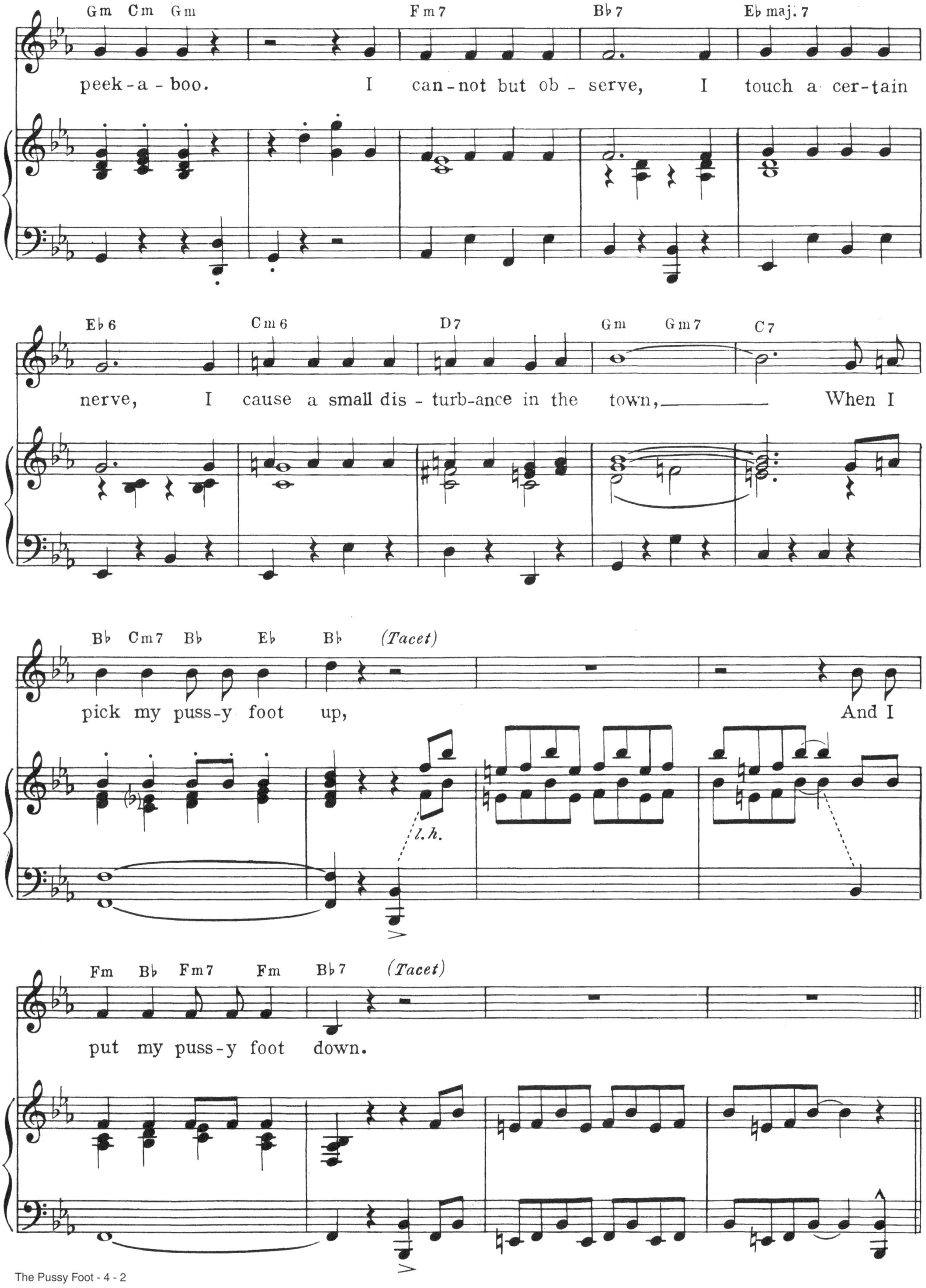
Gm Cm Gm Fm7 Bb7 Eb maj. 7
peek-a-boo. I can-not but ob-serve, I touch a cer-tain
Eb6 Cm6 D7 Gm Gm7 C7
nerve, I cause a small dis-turb-ance in the town, When I
Bb Cm7 Bb Eb Bb (Tacet)
pick my puss-y foot up, And I
l.h.
Fm Bb Fm7 Fm Bb7 (Tacet)
put my puss-y foot down.

Chorus
(Variation)
mp-mf
Bb7 Bb+ Eb6
Ti-ger cats_ tip their hats, Flip their whiskers and purr;
Bb7 F# dim. Eb G7 F G7b5 G7
Pe-kin-ese_ tell their fleas, "Fel-las, fel-las, it's her!"
Cm D7 Gm Bb7 Gm Bb+
It don't be-hoove a la-dy to lie,
Bbm6 C7 Fm7 Bb7 (Tacet)
There is no oth-er kit-ten like I. Strut-tin' down the al-ley,

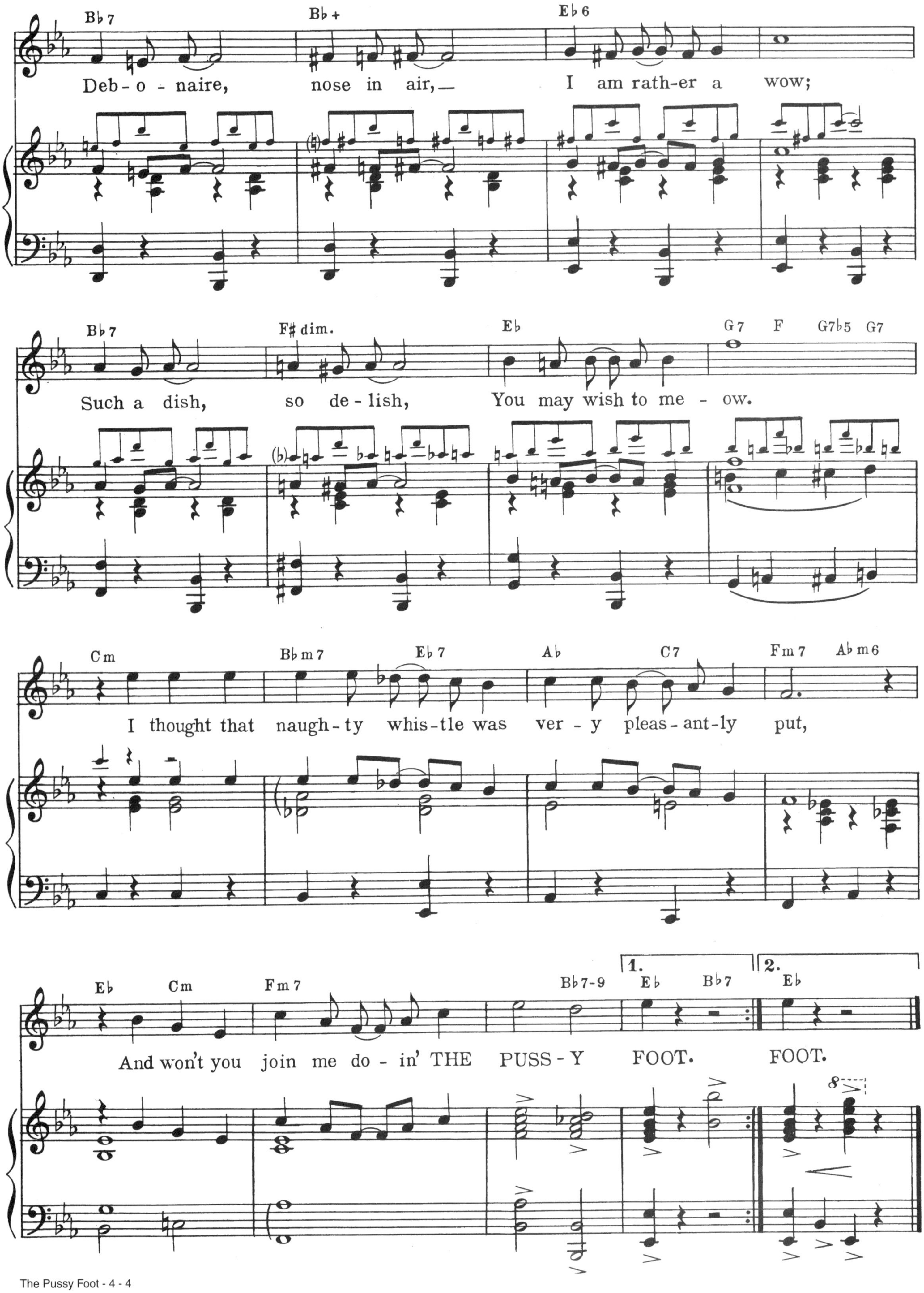
Bb7 Bb+ Eb6
Deb-o-naire, nose in air, I am rath-er a wow;
Bb7 F# dim. Eb G7 F G7b5 G7
Such a dish, so de-lish, You may wish to me-ow.
Cm Bbm7 Eb7 Ab C7 Fm7 Abm6
I thought that naugh-ty whis-tle was ver-y pleas-ant-ly put,
Eb Cm Fm7 Bb7-9 1. Eb Bb7 2. Eb
And won't you join me do-in' THE PUSS-Y FOOT. FOOT.

From the Musical Production "GOLDILOCKS"

SAVE A KISS

Words by
JOAN FORD, JEAN KERR
and WALTER KERR

Music by
LEROY ANDERSON

Allegro
Verse
G D7 E dim. D7 D7♭9 D9 D dim.
One good kiss, you know de- serves an -
mf
mp
mp
Gmaj.7 G6 Gmaj.7 G6 D7♭5 D7 D dim. D7 Gmaj.7
oth - er, And an - oth - er, do you mind?
G6 G B♭ F7 G dim. F7 F7♭9 F9 F dim. B♭maj.7 B♭
I want to keep the first from be - ing lone - ly,
B♭6 Dm B♭ Em7♭5 A+7 A7 D
If you will on - ly be so kind. To -

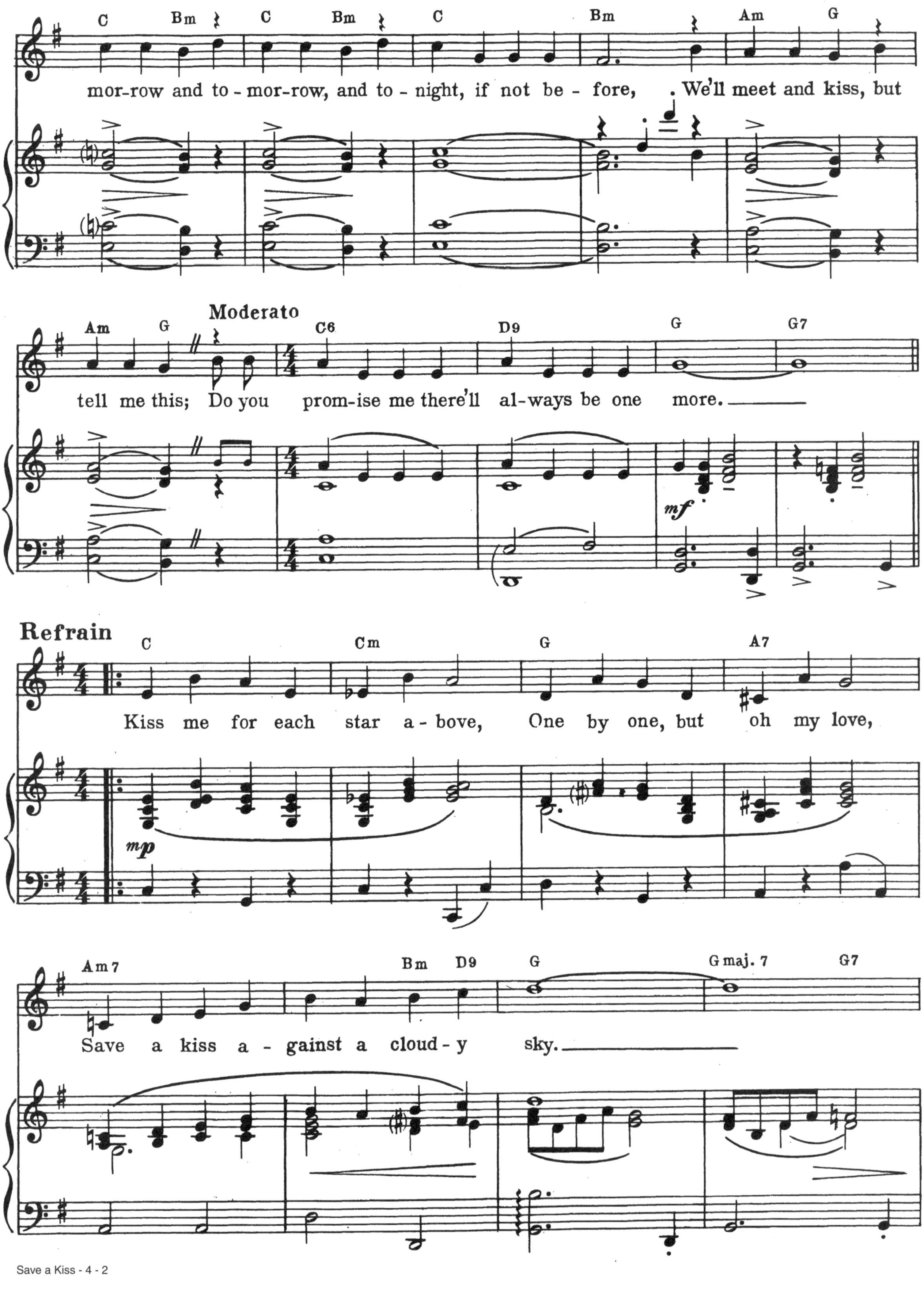
C Bm C Bm C Bm Am G
mor-row and to - mor-row, and to - night, if not be - fore, We'll meet and kiss, but
Am G
Moderato
C6 D9 G G7
tell me this; Do you prom-ise me there'll al-ways be one more.
mf
Refrain
C Cm G A7
Kiss me for each star a - bove, One by one, but oh my love,
mp
Am7 Bm D9 G G maj. 7 G7
Save a kiss a - gainst a cloud - y sky.

C Cm G A7
Sweet and twen - ty kiss - es spend, But re - mem - ber, day dreams end,
Am7 Bm D9 Dm7 G7 Dm7 G7
And a night may come when sweet - hearts sigh.
C Am7 D7 Bm C Bm Bm7 E7 E+ E7
Let's make no mis - take, Lov - ing hearts can break;
Am Am Em7 A7 D7 D9 D7♭9 D7
Put a - way a rain - y day ca - ress.
rall.

G7 G7♭5 G7 G+7 C Cm G
Yes, Kiss me danc - ing, kiss me still, Kiss me now, but
a tempo
A7 Am7 Bm D9
if you will, Save a kiss to save me when I
Bm7♭5 E7 Em7 E7♭5 E7 Am7 Am7 D7♭9
cry, Save a kiss for by - and -
mf
mp
1. 2.
G G Gmaj. 7 G7 G C6 G
by. by.
a tempo
rit.
r. h.

From the Musical Production "GOLDILOCKS"

SHALL I TAKE MY HEART AND GO?

Words by
JOAN FORD, JEAN KERR
and WALTER KERR

Music by
LEROY ANDERSON

Moderato
mf
Verse Allegro
F Bb F Bb C7
I can't de - ny that you're in love, if love is
mf
F F Bb F Bb
blind; With half an eye you would have seen your kiss
mp
A7 D Gm7 Am C+ C7
was kind. If you grew tired of me,

F Dm F+ F G7
you'd tell me so, But you would clear - ly be
Bb Gm7 C7 F
the last to know. Al - low a
mp
Bb F Bb F Bb F Gm7
fool a fool sug - ges - tion, Here's the ques - tion on
f
mp
Moderato
C7 F C7
my mind.
rit.
mf

Chorus
F G7 Gm7 C7 Gm7 C7 F
SHALL I TAKE MY HEART AND GO, my love? Would you
mp-mf
r.h.
D7 D+ D7 Gm Gm7 C9 C7 Am C7 F F7 B♭
ev-er e-ven know my love? Can't you see my dar-ling, what a
A7 Dm F+ Dm7 G7 C7 C
tan-gled web we weave, When we make be-lieve you care?
D♭7 B♭6 A♭ C7 F G7 Gm7 C7 Gm7 C7
If I sim-ply said "good-bye" my love,
mp-mf
r.h.

F D7 D+ D7 Gm Gm7 C9 C7 Am C7 F F7
Would you e - ven won- der why, my love? Though a dream lies
B♭ A7 Dm G9 F Fdim. Gm7 C7 Gm7 C7
dy- ing, I'm the on- ly one who's cry - ing; Dear, if I should wan-der,
rit.
a tempo
Cm6 D7 D+ D7 G7 (sus. C) G7 Gm7 C7
Would your heart grow fond- er, SHALL I TAKE MY HEART AND
1.
2.
F C7 F C7 (sus. F) F
GO? GO?
l.h.
Ped.
*

From the Musical Production "GOLDILOCKS"

THERE NEVER WAS A WOMAN

Words by
JOAN FORD, JEAN KERR
and WALTER KERR

Music by
LEROY ANDERSON

Andante
F Gm7 C7(♭9) F
Com-mon! she says; on the
Gm7 C♯dim7 Dm G F/C D7(♭9) Gm7 C9
make! she says; what I'll nev-er take is the cake, she
Tempo di blues
F6 B♭9 F6 B♭9 F6 B♭9 F6 B♭9 F6 B♭9 F6 B♭9
says. La-dy, you should-n't - a gone and told me what you

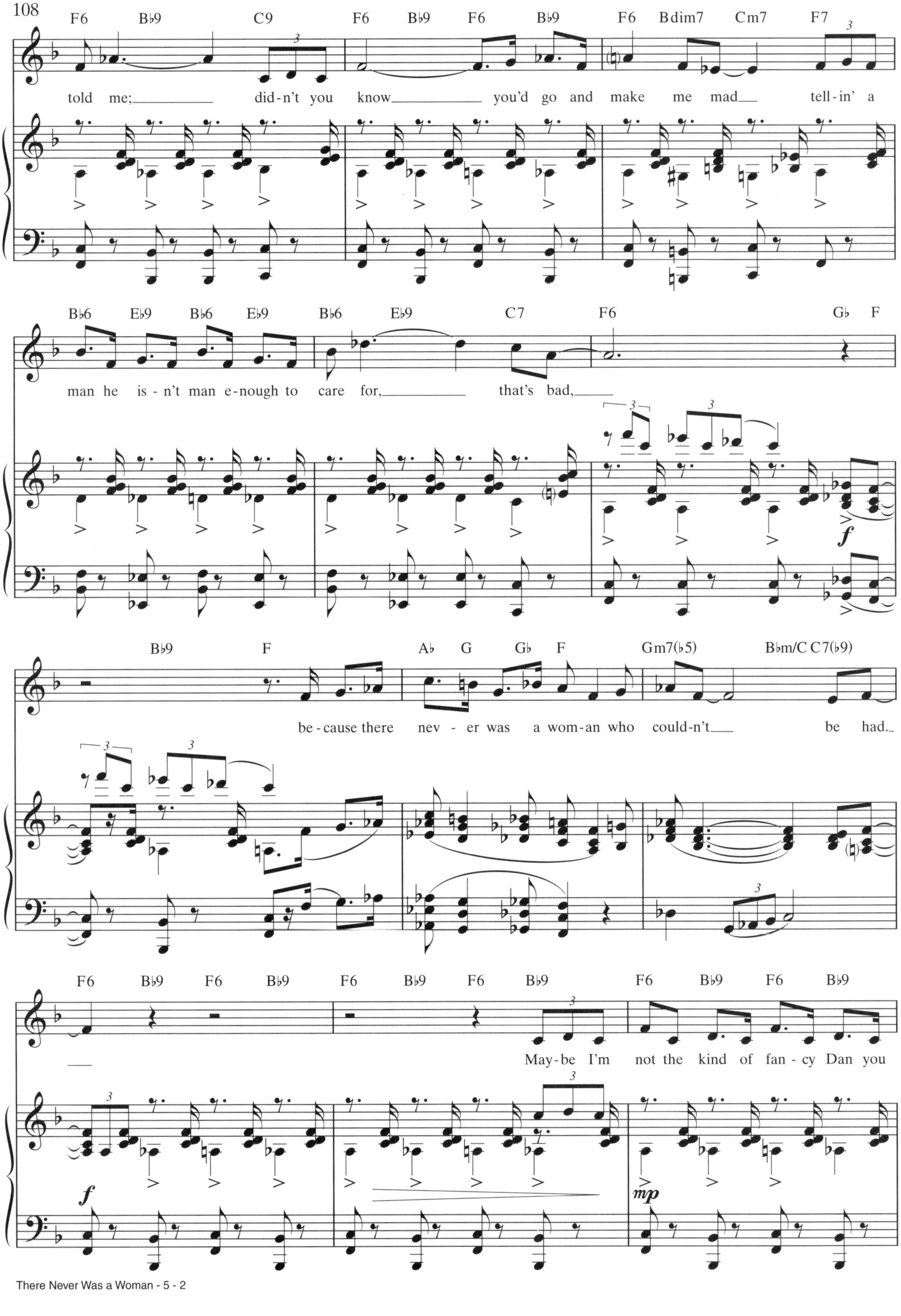
F6 B♭9 C9 F6 B♭9 F6 B♭9 F6 Bdim7 Cm7 F7
told me; did-n't you know you'd go and make me mad tell-in' a
B♭6 E♭9 B♭6 E♭9 B♭6 E♭9 C7 F6 G♭ F
man he is-n't man e-nough to care for, that's bad,
f
B♭9 F A♭ G G♭ F Gm7(♭5) B♭m/C C7(♭9)
be-cause there nev-er was a wom-an who could-n't be had.
F6 B♭9 F6 B♭9 F6 B♭9 F6 B♭9 F6 B♭9 F6 B♭9
May-be I'm not the kind of fan-cy Dan you
f
mp

F6 B♭9 C9 F6 B♭9 F6 B♭9 F6 Bdim7 Cm7 F7
go for; mat-ter of fact, I like a nois - y plaid; mat-ter of
B♭6 E♭9 B♭6 E♭9 B♭6 E♭9 C7 F6 G♭ F
fact, you'd nev - er take me for no high - tone col - lege grad;
B♭9 F A♭ G G♭ F Gm7(♭5) B♭m/C C7(♭9)
but still there nev - er was a wom - an who could - n't be had.
F6 B♭9 F6 B♭9 F6 B♭9 F6 B♭ B♭maj7
Tell me I'm mean, green,

B♭6 Bdim7 F/C Cm7 F7
ought-ta be kept in quar-an-tine and I'll nev-er bat an eye. La-dy, be
B♭m B♭m(maj7) B♭m7 E♭7 A♭
smart, start look-in' for plac-es to hide your heart or you'll be my val - en -
C7 F6 B♭9 F6 B♭9 F6 B♭9 C9
tine. Should-n't have told me I could nev-er make you tin-gle, la-dy, look
mp
F6 B♭9 F6 B♭9 F6 Bdim7 Cm7 F7 B♭6 E♭9 B♭6 E♭9
out! I'm not Sir Gal - a-had, la-dy, look out! I'm just an or-di-nar-y

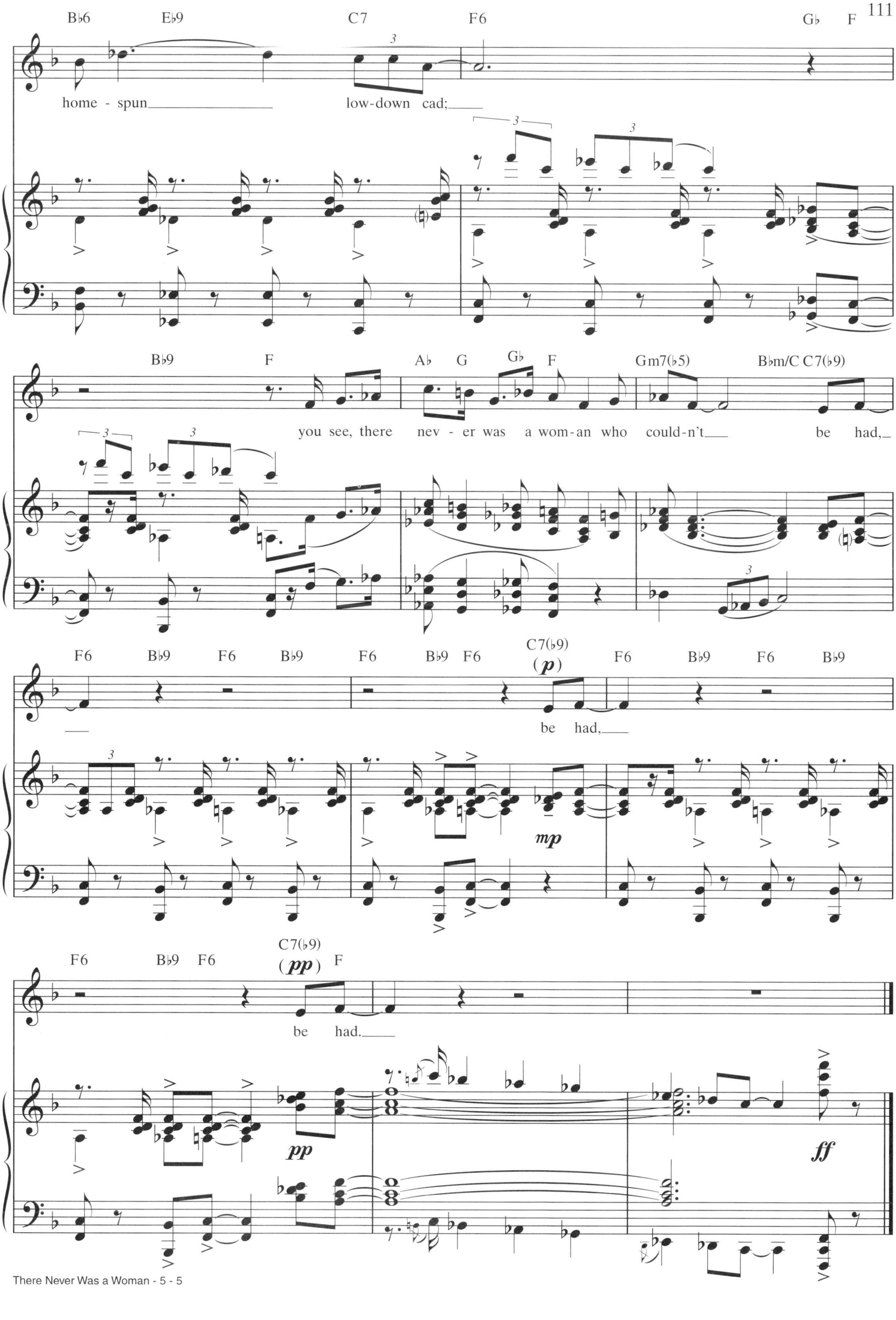

B♭6 E♭9 C7 F6 G♭ F
home - spun low-down cad;
B♭9 F A♭ G G♭ F Gm7(♭5) B♭m/C C7(♭9)
you see, there nev - er was a wom-an who could-n't be had,
F6 B♭9 F6 B♭9 F6 B♭9 F6 C7(♭9) F6 B♭9 F6 B♭9
(p)
be had,
mp
F6 B♭9 F6 C7(♭9) F
(pp)
be had.
pp
ff

From the Musical Production "GOLDILOCKS"

TWO YEARS IN THE MAKING

Words by
JOAN FORD, JEAN KERR
and WALTER KERR

Music by
LEROY ANDERSON

Moderately bright
B♭ Gm B♭/D Cm/E♭
B♭/F B♭dim7/F F7
B♭ E♭ Cm F7 B♭ Gm C7
Two years in the mak - ing, two years on the
F F7 B♭ B♭maj7 B♭7 E♭maj7 Cm7(♭5)
way; the pic-ture they said could nev-er be made is

B♭/F Dm/F F7 B♭ F C7/E
gon - na be made to - day. See it now, an ep - ic theme!
F/E♭ B♭/D F/C Dm Gm7 C7 F Dm7 G+ G7 Cm
See it now, a dar-ing first! Un-for-get-ta-ble, un-sur-passed, un - a-shamed, un - re-hearsed.
F C7/E F/E♭ B♭/D F/C Dm7 Gm7 C7
Torn be-tween a moth-er's knee, tempt-ed by un - bri-dled lust; bring the kid-dies, fun for all.
F Gm7/F F B♭/F F7 B♭ E♭ Cm F7
It's a - maz-ing, it's a must! Two years in the mak - ing,

B♭ Gm C7 F F7 B♭ B♭maj7
two years on the way; the pic-ture they said could
B♭7 E♭maj7 Cm7(♭5) B♭/F Dm/F F7 B♭
nev-er be made is gon-na be made to-day.
G5 D/G
See in-side E-gyp-tian tem-ples, see what real-ly goes on.
G5 D/G G5 C5
See al-lur-ing vir-gins with hard-ly an-y clothes on. See the flash-ing i-dol eat-ing

G/C
C5
F7
maid-ens for a hob-by. See the i-dol eat them up, doc-tor's in the lob-by.
B♭
E♭
Cm
F7
B♭
Gm
C7
Two years in the mak-ing, two years on the
F
F7
B♭
B♭maj7
B♭7
E♭maj7
Cm7(♭5)
way; the pic-ture they said could nev-er be made is
B♭/F
Dm/F
F7
B♭
gon-na be made to-day.

F7
B♭
B♭dim
B♭/F
Why is this one of the truly great films of our time?
F7
B♭
C7
F
It is first of all a love story, a stolen kiss their only crime, a simple story of pagan joy. Not since Mother Fergusson's boy such
N.C.
courage - raw, fury - savage, passion - searing, action - pounding,
Fdim7
F7
churning, pulsing, thundering, throbbing and loaded
with chuckles.
cresc.
f

(Pantomime)
B♭m
G♭
mf
C7
8vb
Fm
B♭m6
Fm/C
C7
F
B♭
E♭
Cm
F7
B♭
Gm
C7
Two years in the mak - ing, two years on the
F
F7
B♭
B♭maj7
B♭7
E♭maj7
Cm7(♭5)
way; the pic-ture they said could nev-er be made is

B♭/F
Dm/F
F7
B♭
gon - na be made to - day.
C
C7
F5
E - gypt. E - gypt. E - G - Y - P - T.
See the cam - els, see the slave girls,
See. See.
D♭/F
see the hand - some he - ro save girls.
See. See.

Fm6
See the i - dol, see the or - a - cle. Hys -
See.
See.
A♭7/C
C7
F
ter - i - cal. His - tor - i - cal.
B♭
E♭
Cm
F7
B♭
Two years in the mak - ing, two
Gm
C7
F
F7
B♭
B♭maj7
years on the way; the pic - ture they said could

B♭7 E♭maj7 Cm7(♭5) B♭/F Dm/F F♯dim7 Gm
nev - er be made is gon - na be made to - day,
Am/C C7 B♭/F F♯/F G/F
Cast of thousands.
Runs for minutes.
An emotional typhoon.
and it's com - ing, com - ing, com - ing,
Fm7 F B♭
Watch for it!
Watch out for it!
com - ing,
Gm E♭6 B♭/D Cm7 B♭
com - ing to your neigh - bor - hood soon.
rall.

From the Musical Production "GOLDILOCKS"

WHO'S BEEN SITTING IN MY CHAIR?

Words by
JOAN FORD, JEAN KERR
and WALTER KERR

Music by
LEROY ANDERSON

Allegretto
F (no 3rd)
F
When Gol - di - locks went vis - i - ting the bears, they
mf
p
B♭/F F B♭/F C/F F
Dm
came home from the fo - rest un - a - wares, found cu - shions off the chairs,
Dm B7 Am/E E♭dim7 Bdim7 Am
Por - ridge ev'- ry wheres, and bed - lam in the bed - room when they hur - ried up the stairs. When
stringendo
p
f
pp
a tempo
Fm
A♭ D♭ A♭ E♭ A♭ D♭ A♭
(sadly)
(primly)
I come home, I look a - round and sigh. Ev - 'ry thing is neat as ap - ple pie. A

a tempo
broadly-rall
B♭m6 Gm7(♭5) B♭m6 Gm7(♭5) C Gm7 C Gm7 C Gm7 C7 B♭/C C7
char-ming lit-tle nest, It gets me so de-pressed, I want to die. Know why?
mf
F B♭6 C7 Dm Gm/B♭ B♭dim F
mf Who's been sit-ting in my chair? Just me. Just me.
3
F B♭6 C7 Dm Gm6 A+7 Dm Gm7(♭5)/D♭
Seems such a pi-ty when I'd share it wil - ing - ly.
F/C F7 B♭ A7/G F/A Dm G7 G9
I want a den that is hap-py, hom-ey, I've got a yen for a lap be-low me.

F/C F7 B♭ F♯dim7 Gm D7/A B♭6 C
If you were sit-ting in my chair, oh, gosh, oh, gee.
F B♭6 C7 Dm Gm/B♭ B♭dim F
Who's been eat-ing my por-ridge? Just me, that's who.
F B♭6 C7 Dm Gm6 A+7 Dm Gm7(♭5)/D♭
I'm just the type to go for-ag-ing for a mid-night snack for two. When you
F/C F7 B♭ A7/G F/A Dm G7 G9
don't see a soul with your morn-ing cof-fee, you can't cas-se-role and you can't pull tof-fee.

F/C F7 B♭ F♯dim7 Gm C7(♭9) F
If you were eat-ing my por-ridge, oh dear, oh do.
B♭6 C9 F6 Gm/E A7 Dm
Heigh - ho and lack - a - day, a lack of love will turn me gray.
B♭6 C9 F6 G7sus4/D G9 C G7 C
I'd like to run a - way, just like Gol - di - locks.
F B♭6 C7 Dm Gm/B♭ B♭dim F
Who's been sleep- ing in my bed? Just me, just "moi."

F Bb6 C7 Dm Gm/E A+ Dm G7(b5)/Db
I'd like a two fis - ted bi - ped in my bou - doir.
F/C F7 Bb A7/G F/A Dm G7 G9
I'd like a tweed hang - ing next to that dress. I'd like to need a lar - ger mat - tress.
F/C F7 Bb A7(b9) Dm F+7 Bb D7(b9) Gm C7
If you were sleep - ing in my bed, tra - la, tra - la, tra - la, tra -
f
F Bb/C F Bb/C F Bb/C F
la. Tra - la!
mf

Cut from the Musical Production "GOLDILOCKS"

COME TO ME

(Go and Catch a Falling Star)

Words by
JOAN FORD, JEAN KERR
and WALTER KERR

Music by
LEROY ANDERSON

G F/G G7 G7sus4 G7
mp Shall we pre -
mp dolce
Cmaj7 C7 F A7
tend as friend to friend you're not en - chant-ed with a hun-dred hap-py dreams I'll nev-er
Dm7 G7 Cmaj7 C7 Fmaj7
share? Shall we pre- tend that you don't take my heart for grant - ed, That you
D7/A D7 G E♭7 A♭ E♭7sus4 E♭
care, that you care? mf It's a love-ly game we're play-ing_ and there's a
mf
colla voca

A♭/C A♭ B♭7/G♯ E♭/G B♭ E♭ G/D D/A G
chance that one night late you'll blink your eyes and re - al - ize we
a tempo
Dm/F Dm7 G7/F C(♭5) C/G C(♭5) C/G
serve who stand and wait.
poco allarg.
a tempo
Refrain C(♭5) C/G C(♭5) C/G G9(♭5) G7
mp
Go and catch a fall - ing star, bind it in your
G9(♭5) G7 Cm C/G Cm C/G
hair, gath er all the dreams there are,

Gm7/D G7(♭9) Gm7/D G7 Bm/F♯ Am
cresc.
Find them pass - ing fair. I want the world to
cresc.
E7sus4/B E7 Am G♯m/B E
see the girl I love in all her charms
Em Am7 C/D Bm/D G7
See the girl I love with ros - es trem - bling in her arms.
mp
cresc.
G7 C(♭5) C/G C(♭5) C/G
allarg.
a tempo
I don't want to change a note
mp

G9(♭5) G7 G9(♭5) G7 Cm C/G
of___ the song you sing. Long___ a- go a
Cm C/G Gm7/D G7(♭9) Gm7/D G7(♭9)
po - et wrote "Who___ can tame the spring?" So
Am C7/G C7 F
dance___ the night a - way___ un - til your heart is glow- ing
cresc.
D9 Bm D7 C a tempo Cmaj7 Gm7/C
o - ver flow - ing, Should___ the joy and laugh - ter grow
f allarg.
p a tempo

Fmaj7
Fm(maj7)
Am G F
pale the morn - ing aft - er then come
Fm E♭ D♭
1.
C(♭5) C/G C(♭5) C/G
to
me
2.
C(♭5) C/G C(♭5) C/G C(♭5) C/G C
me
Ped.

Cut from the Musical Production "GOLDILOCKS"

GUESS WHO

Words by
JOAN FORD, JEAN KERR
and WALTER KERR

Music by
LEROY ANDERSON

Brightly
mf
Verse
Maggie:
C7 F Bb F C7 F C7 F C7 F Bb F Bb F
The way I'm feel-ing, you could sweep me off the ceil-ing; I'm wild, I'm reel - ing, I'm
mp
Bb F Bb C7 F Bb F C7 F A7 Dm C G7 C
waltz-ing on air. I'm so cy - clon-ic, you could bot-tle me for ton-ic. I'm frank-ly his-tri-
G C6 G7 C G7 Dm7 G7 C Bb C7 Gm7 C Gm7 C7
on-ic and frank-ly, I don't care, don't care, don't care!

Refrain

C7 Fmaj. 7 Am7 D7-9 Gm7 C7-9 C7
GUESS WHO is wear-ing pink this Spring, Who can't think this Spring, who's a -
mp-mf
Fmaj. 7 F6 Gm7 C7 F maj. 7 Am7 D7-9
glow. GUESS WHO be-lieves in dreams a lit -
Gm7 C7-9 C7 F9 F6 A F7 Bb Gm7 C7
- tle, Who seems a lit - tle bit slow. And GUESS WHO los -
Gm7 C7 Am7 F D7 D7+5 Gm7 G9 G7 Gm7 C9 C7
- es um - brel - las And who puts salt in her tea. When

F maj. 7
Am7
D7-9
Gm7
C7-9
C7
Cu - - pid's lit-tle dart went off, Guess whose heart went off on a
Cm6
D7+5
D7-9
Gm7
C7
Gm7
C7
1. Repeat - Optional
F
Gm7
C7
spree. Who's in love? I guess that it's me! GUESS
mf
2.
F
Fine
To Interlude
F
Girls
Gm7
C7
me! me! Cross your heart now, Mag-gie, hon-ey, Would you
Fine
mf
Gm7
C7
D (add E)
D
D maj. 7
love him if he weren't a mil-lion - aire?
f

Maggie:
D Dm7 G7 Dm7 G7
I re - spect him for his mon- ey, But I love him for his love-ly sa-voir
mf
A(add E) A A maj. 7 A
Girls (spoken)
C7
faire.
There you'll be, the
f
p
F6 C7 F E7 Am
op - er - a, the vil - la by the sea, Can-dle-light and call-ing cards, the
(Opt.)
G C
Maggie:
C Gm7 C Dm D♯dim. C
D.S. al Fine
C7
bish-op in to tea. It's me, it's mag - ic, It's more than I can bear! GUESS
mf
D.S. al Fine

Cut from the Musical Production "GOLDILOCKS"

HE'LL NEVER STRAY

Words by
JOAN FORD, JEAN KERR
and WALTER KERR

Music by
LEROY ANDERSON

Tempo di Rhumba

Cm
G7
The
Cm Bb F Cm/Eb G+ Cm G7
day a girl mar-ries the man of her choice, we
Cm F Cm/Eb G+ Cm
say is le - git - i - mate cause to re - joice. But when-
Dm7 G7 Cmaj7 C6 Dm7 G7 F/G Cmaj7 C
ev-er you go to a wed- ding, the min-ute the knot is tied, if you

B7 Em A13 A7(♭5)
lis-ten you hear___ sobs from the rear___ they come from the friends of the bride. They
Cm B♭ F Cm/E♭ G+ Cm
know__ as they toss her a hand-ful of rice___ that a
Fm6 Cm/E♭ Fm6 Cm/E♭ D7sus4/A D7 G7
man is-n't true just from say-ing, "I do." they should toss in a lit-tle ad-vice. If you
Cmaj7 C6 Cmaj7 C7
get your vi-chy-ssoises chil-ly, if your cof-fee's hot as can be. If you

F7
G7
mix a hef-ty high-ball and a light souf-fle, he'll ne-ver stray. If you
Cmaj7
C6
Cmaj7
C7
scrub the floor with a flou-rish; if you starch his shirts to a "T" If you
F7
G7
C7 C+7
keep the girl-ish gla-mour of your wed-ding day, he'll ne-ver stray Oh, he
F
C
F
C
might wink once at a red head; he might look twice at a blond; light

Fm
Cm/E♭
D♭7
A♭7 G7
cig - a - rettes for tall bru-nettes,but would he wan-der if he could? He would! If you
Cmaj7
C6
Cmaj7
C7
clamp a chain on his an - kle, and you hitch a ball on the chain; if you
F7
G7
lock him in thebarn and throw the key a - way, then there's a chance
G7 F/G G7 C
He'll ne - ver stray

Cut from the Musical Production "GOLDILOCKS"

HELLO

Words by
JOAN FORD, JEAN KERR
and WALTER KERR

Music by
LEROY ANDERSON

Andante

C♯dim7 Dm7 Fmaj7 B♭maj7 C9 C7(♭9) F6
mf
mp
It was a
C9/F F6 C9/F F(add9) F A♭ B♭
strange night from the be-gin-ning, strange and sweet; A star fell, I
F(add9) Fmaj7 F A♭ C7 Dm7 G7 C7sus4 C7
think, and I fell, I think, right at your feet. Hel-
poco rit.
p
F6 F♯dim7 D7(♭9)/F♯ Gm E7/G♯ Am7 Fmaj7/A A+
lo, well, now bless my eyes! It's you, what a nice sur-prise!

Hello - 3 - 1

B♭ F/C Dm7 Em/G G7 C7sus4 C7 C9 C7
One glance and I'm danc-ing thru the skies. Hel-
F6 F♯dim7 D7(♭9)/F♯ Gm E/G♯ Am7 Fmaj7/A A+
lo do you un-der-stand how I bare-ly touched your hand,
B♭ F/C Dm7 Em/G G7 Csus4 C C(omit3,add2) C
and felt I dwelt in a won-der-land Dear
f
A♭ B♭ F(add2) F Fmaj7 Gm7 C7 C♯dim7/F F
Heart, my own it's true that love out-wits you; I

A♭ B♭ F(add2) F Dm G7sus4 G7 C9 C7(♭9) C7
should have known you nev-er see the one that hits you. Hel -
F6 F♯dim7 D7(♭9)/F♯ Gm E7/G♯ Am Fmaj7/A A+ B♭ F/C
lo, did I star-tle you? You know what a heart'-ll do: skip once and
Dm7 Em/G G7 B♭maj7 B♭6 Dm7/G C(add9) C♯dim7 Dm Fmaj7
then skip a life - time through. Hel - lo, my
B♭maj7 C9
1. F6 F/A Gm7 C C7
2. F6 A♭ B♭ F A♭ B♭ F
love, Hel- lo. Hel - lo.
mf
p

Cut from the Musical Production "GOLDILOCKS"

IF I CAN'T TAKE IT WITH ME

Words by
JOAN FORD, JEAN KERR
and WALTER KERR

Music by
LEROY ANDERSON

Andante Moderato
n.c.
B♭
B♭7
E♭6/B♭
There's a place that I would some day
semplice
mp
Fm/B♭
A♭/B♭
B♭
Cm/B♭
Fm7
B♭
E♭maj7
A♭
like to call my own, with win-dows wide, a lamp in-side a
Cm7 sus
Cm7
Dm/F
F7
B♭9sus4
B♭
B♭
B♭7
E♭6/B♭
key for me a - lone. it's all I want in this wide, wide world, I
cresc.

Fm/B♭ A♭/B♭ Gm7 E♭/G Cm7 F7 B♭/F Adim Ddim
might as well be frank. I want my own, my ve - ry own,
Allegro
Cm7 F9 B♭7 B♭7sus4/C C♯m6 B♭7
First Na - tional Bank. Dad - dy
E♭ Gm/B♭ Fm7 B♭7 E♭ Gm/B♭ Fm7 B♭7
I'm all set to pam - per and pet my mon - ey. I can
E♭ Gm/B♭ Fm7 B♭7 E♭ Gm/B♭ Gm7(♭5) C7
hard - ly wait to cud - dle that do - si - do. You can

Fm7 C7 Fm7
call me sen - ti - men - tal or call me fun - ny, Hon - ey. But if I
Cm7 F7 Fm6 Edim7 Fm6 E♭/A B♭7
can't take it with me, I'm not gon - na go. When the
E♭ Gm/B♭ Fm7 B♭7 E♭ Gm/B♭ Fm7 B♭7
win - ter comes I'll bun - dle it to Mi - am - i Want to
E♭ Gm/B♭ Fm7 B♭7 E♭ Gm/B♭ Gm7(♭5) C7
give those sil - ver dol - lars a gold - en glow. I'll sit

Fm7 C7 Fm7
up at night and pol - ish 'em with a cha - mois, Lamb - y___ and if I
F7 B♭9 E♭6 A♭6 Adim7 E♭6
can't take it with me, I'm not gon - na go.___ There were
G♭ B♭7/F E♭ G♭ B♭7/F E♭
days when the cup-board was bare___ and I had - n't the will to suc - ceed,__ but I
G♭ B♭/F E♭ Cm7 F7 B♭
spoken:
ne - ver gave in_ to des - pair_ and I held_ to my creed:__ "Simple Greed!" if you

E♭ Gm/B♭ Fm7 B♭7 E♭ Gm/B♭ Fm7 B♭7
buy the pitch the woes_ of the rich are weight-y.________ Well if
E♭ Gm/B♭ Fm7 B♭7 E♭ Gm/B♭ Gm7(♭5) C7
I could choose my mis - er - y here be - low________ I'd be
Fm C7 Fm Adim7
good and rich and mis - 'ra-ble till I'm eight-ty______ Mat-ey__ And if I
1.
E♭/B♭ Fm7 B♭7 E♭ B♭7
can't take it with me I'm not gon-na go._ Dad- dy

2.
E♭/B♭ Cm Fm7 A♭6 B♭7 B♭7/D
can't take it with me, I'm not gon - na
E♭ E♭7/D♭ A♭7/C B7(♭5) A♭/B♭ E♭maj7
go.
8vb

Cut from the Musical Production "GOLDILOCKS"

LITTLE GIRLS SHOULD BE SEEN

Words by
JOAN FORD, JEAN KERR
and WALTER KERR

Music by
LEROY ANDERSON

Allegro

C(omit3)
C(omit3)
The world a - bounds in
Cmaj7(omit3rd)
C7(omit3rd)
sights and sounds that make my sens - es whirl, They
F/C
Fm/C
C
whirl the most when I am close to some en - chant - ing
D7/A
F♯m7
B7
Em
Em(maj7)
girl. For girls are na - ture's glo - ry And
f

Em7 A7 Dm A7 Dm7
girls are man's de - light, As a man who has stud- ied the
sfz
Dm7 Am/E Dm Cmaj7 F/A G9 G7 C/G G7 C/G G9
ev - i - dence I ad - mit they're a bit of all right
(spoken)
But!
C7 Cmaj7/G C7 Cmaj7/G
1. Lit - tle
C7 Cmaj7/G C7 Cmaj7/G C7 Cmaj7/G
1: girls should be seen and not mar - ried, Lit - tle girls should be wooed but not
2: girls should be seen and not mar - ried, Lit - tle girls should be tamed but not

C9 Fmaj9 G/C C Fm6 C6/G Am7
wed;___ The most del - i - cate blos - som is play - ing o - pos - sum till
took;___ The most trem - u - lous flow - er is lust - ing for pow - er un -
C/D D7 C/D D7 G C7 C+7 F F6 B♭maj7/F F
she gets a lease on your bed,___ Then she chang - es, How she
til you are safe on the hook.___ Then she chang - es, How she
Em/G Am7/E Am7/E Em F F(add9) G7 Gm6/B♭ A7 F/A C/G
chang - es! How she takes you when she takes your name!___ As you're
chang - es! How she seems to be what she is not!___ When she
Dm7 G7 Cmaj7 C6/G Dm7 G7
leav - ing the church you are bust - ing with pride, you don't know the min - ute you
prom - ised to serve you with pleas - ure and praise, she meant she'd be hap - py the

Cmaj7 C6/G Dm7 G9 Gm6/B♭ A7
made her your bride your dar-ling Miss Je- kyll be - came Mis - sis Hyde. It's a
rest of her days just cook -ing your goose and mend-ing your ways, it's a
D7 F♯dim7 C/G Adim7
shame! It's a shame! Lit - tle girls, lit - tle
plot! It's a plot!
C/G Adim7 C/G B♭/D B♭ B♭/F B♭/D B♭ G7
girls, lit - tle girls should be seen and not
1. C Cmaj7 C7 Cmaj7
wed. 2: Lit - tle

2
C6
wed.
Oh, I
G7/C
C6
G7/C
may be a faint heart-ed lov - er.
But I've learned in my bach - e - lor
C6
B7
Em
Am7
life:
You can't tell a book by its cov-er,
Scratch an - y
D7
C/D
D7
G7
C7
Cmaj7/G
C7
Cmaj7/G
girl, you'll dis-cov - er a wife.
3: Lit-tle

C7 Cmaj7/G C7 Cmaj7/G C7 Cmaj7/G
3: girls should be seen and not mar - ried,______ Lit - tle girls should be kissed and not
4: girls should be seen and not mar - ried.______ Lit - tle girls should be wooed and not
C7 Fmaj9 G/C C Fm6 C6/G Am7
kept;________ The most pas- sion- ate peach- es are stoned heart- ed crea- tures, a
wed;________ The most scat - ter- brain nif - ty is bas - i- c'lly shift - y, At
C/D D7 C/D D7 G C7 C+7 F F6 B♭maj7/F F
truth that is hard to ac - cept.__________ For she chang - es, How she
six she was plan- ning a - head.__________ For she chang - es, How she
Em/G Am7/E Am7/E F F(add9) G7 Gm6/B♭ A7 F/A C/G
chang - es! How she turns from your ea - ger ca - ress!______ Now sup -
chang - es! And the main thing she chang - es is you!______ On the

Dm7 G7 Cmaj7 C6/G Dm7 G7
pose you've been mar-ried for less than a year, You're snug by the fire and you're
day you are wed you're a light heart-ed lad, The next thing you no-tice she's
Cmaj7 C6/G Dm7 G Gm/B♭ A7
hold-ing her near, she sighs and she mur-murs "Is the gar-bage out, dear?" It's a
knit-ting like mad, you kissed her and Mis-ter, You're now dear old Dad. Oh, it's
D7 F♯dim7 C/G Adim7 C/G Adim7
mess! It's a mess! lit-tle girls, girls,
true! All too true
1.
C/G B♭/D B♭ B♭/F B♭/D B♭ G7 C Cmaj7/G C7 Cmaj7/G
girls should be seen and not wed.
4: Lit-tle

2.
C/G
B♭/D
B♭
B♭/D
B♭
B♭/F
B♭/D
B♭
B♭/F
girls should be seen
B♭/D
G7
C
Dm/G
C
Dm/G
C
Dm/B
Em/A
and not wed.
Fm/A♭
G♭/A♭
A♭7
D♭
G7
C

Cut from the Musical Production "GOLDILOCKS"

MY LAST SPRING

Words by
JOAN FORD, JEAN KERR
and WALTER KERR

Music by
LEROY ANDERSON

Allegro
Eb/Bb Bb7 Eb/Bb Bb7(no3rd) Eb/Bb Bb7
I've had the birds, I've had the bees, I've
f
mf
(with pedal)
Eb7 Ab Bb9/Ab Eb/G Bb7/F Eb F7 Bb
had 'em and I've had 'em. I've let the li - lacs stir in me an urge as old as Ad - am. Let a
Eb/Bb Bb7(no3rd) Eb7 Ab Bb9/Ab Eb/G Adim7
rall.
sin - gle blade of grass ap - pear and this sil - ly heart would soft - en. But now I know, oh,
rall.
Andante tranquillo
Eb/Bb Cm7 Fm C7/G Fm/Ab Adim7 Eb/Bb Bb7(b9) Eb6
how I know I've been to the dog - wood once too of - ten.

Refrain:
Eb6
Eb6 Bb Eb6
Db/Eb Eb7
A - pril, dear, I see your lit - tle game. Ev - 'ry year the same old thing.
Ab Abm6 Bb6 C Fm7 Gm/F Bb7 Bbm6/Db Dbm6
Up the path go Jack and Joan, you know who comes back a - lone.
Eb/F F7 Fm7/Bb Bb7(b9) Eb6
This is my last spring. Blue - birds, sweet, we
Bbm7/Eb Eb7 Ab Abm6
must - n't meet a - gain. Should we meet, you must - n't sing. Bon voy - age and

B♭6 C Fm7 Gm B♭7 B♭m6/D♭ D♭m6 E♭/F F7 Fm7/B♭ B♭7(♭9)
too - dle - oo, don't call me, I won't call you. This is my last
Poco più animato
E♭6 Fm B♭9 E♭maj7 E♭6
spring. The daf - fo - dils on the hills
Fm7 A♭/B♭ B♭7 E♭ Cm N.C. F7
have on - ly made me cry. Heav-en knows I'll miss them, just the same I'll kiss them good -
Tempo I
B♭7 rall. E♭6
bye. Coun - try ways are all de - sert - ed now,
rall.

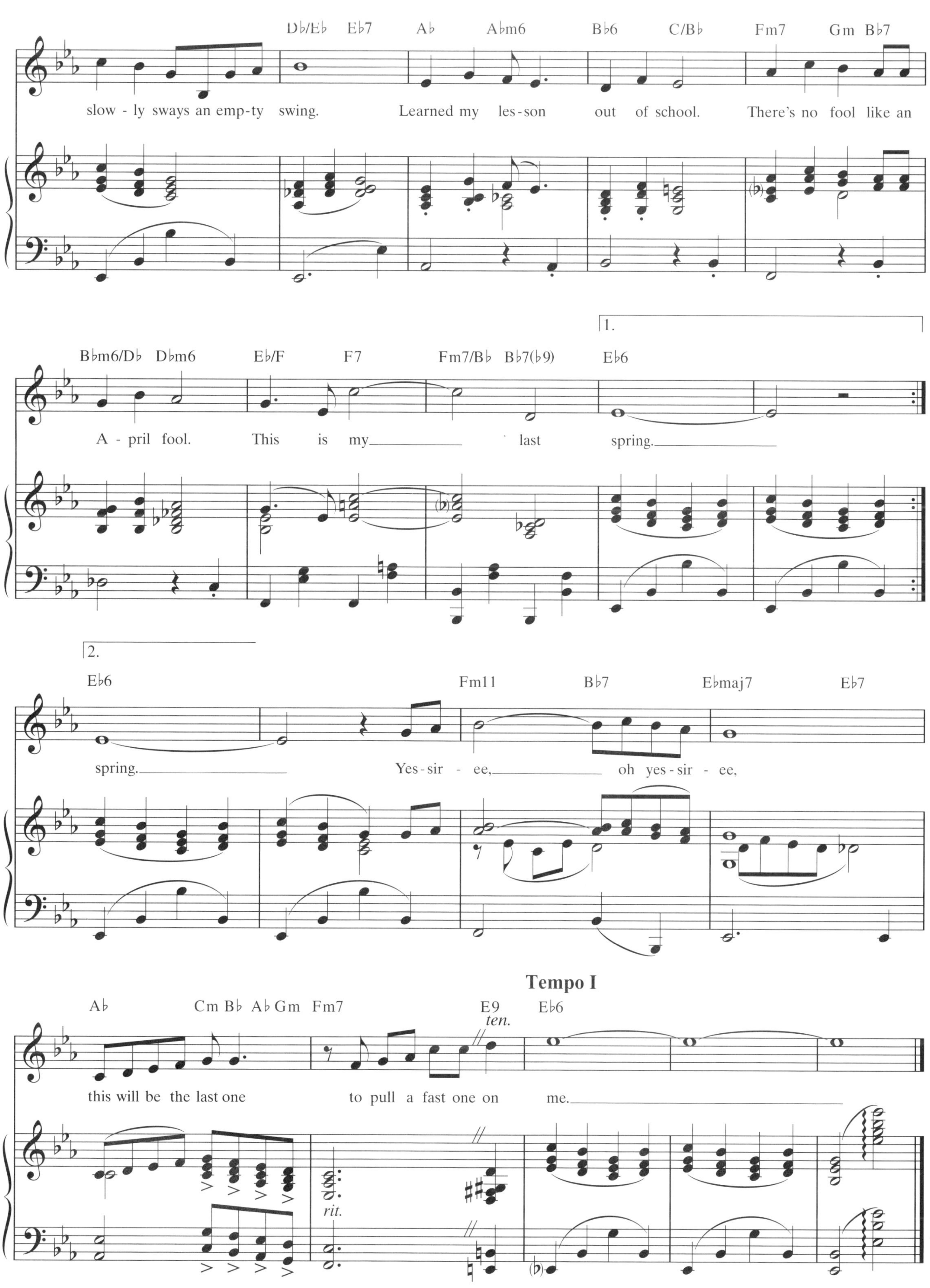
D♭/E♭ E♭7 A♭ A♭m6 B♭6 C/B♭ Fm7 Gm B♭7
slow - ly sways an emp-ty swing. Learned my les-son out of school. There's no fool like an
B♭m6/D♭ D♭m6 E♭/F F7 Fm7/B♭ B♭7(♭9) E♭6
1.
A - pril fool. This is my last spring.
2.
E♭6 Fm11 B♭7 E♭maj7 E♭7
spring. Yes-sir - ee, oh yes-sir - ee,
Tempo I
A♭ Cm B♭ A♭ Gm Fm7 E9 E♭6
ten.
this will be the last one to pull a fast one on me.
rit.

Cut from the Musical Production "GOLDILOCKS"

TAGALONG KID

Words by
JOAN FORD, JEAN KERR
and WALTER KERR

Music by
LEROY ANDERSON

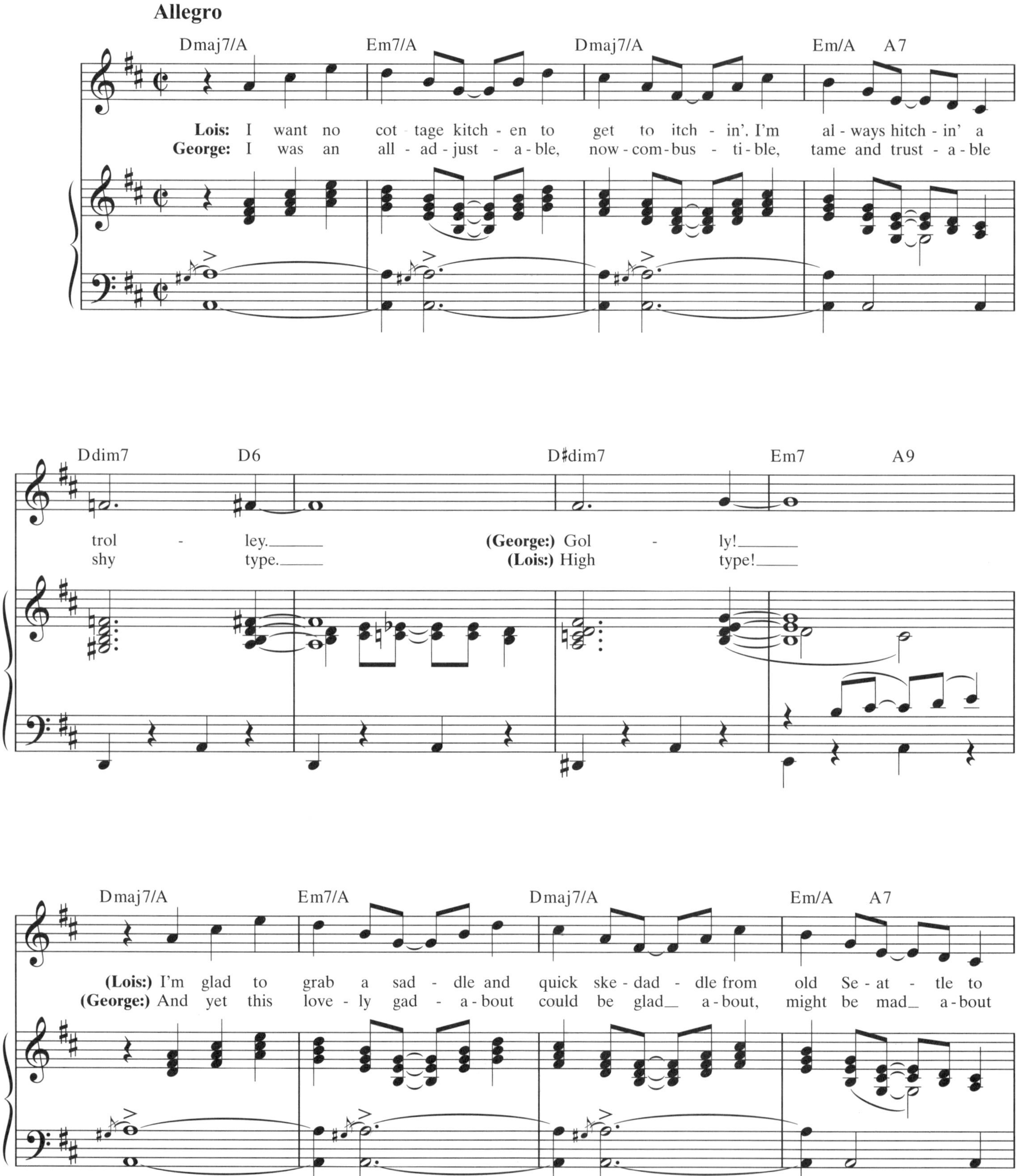
Allegro
Dmaj7/A Em7/A Dmaj7/A Em/A A7
Lois: I want no cot - tage kitch - en to get to itch - in'. I'm al - ways hitch - in' a
George: I was an all - ad - just - a - ble, now - com - bus - ti - ble, tame and trust - a - ble
Ddim7 D6 D♯dim7 Em7 A9
trol - ley. (George:) Gol - ly!
shy type. (Lois:) High type!
Dmaj7/A Em7/A Dmaj7/A Em/A A7
(Lois:) I'm glad to grab a sad - dle and quick ske - dad - dle from old Se - at - tle to
(George:) And yet this love - ly gad - a - bout could be glad_ a - bout, might be mad_ a - bout

F♯m
G♯m
C♯7
F♯m7
G♯m7
C♯7
Ba - li.
my type.
(George:) Jol - ly!
(Lois:) Thy type.
F♯m
Bm6/F♯
F♯m7
B9
(Lois:) What is this wan - der - lust that I must o - bey?
(George:) I know the way it feels to be tem - pest tossed.
Str.
Cls.
Em
Am6/E
Em7
Em/A
A7(♭9)
It's just that if I hes - i - tate he might get a -
I'm al - ways at her heels to be sure I don't get
D
2nd time To Coda I
G/A
A7
Dmaj9
D6
way.
lost.
In a rick - et - y rick - shaw, in a leak - y ca -
Cls.

Em11 G/A A7 Dmaj9 D6 G6 Dmaj9 D6
noe, in a chol - e - ra scare, I'll be there, I'll be
F♯m7 Fdim7 Em7 A9
true. I'll trail him by yacht or by yak, I'll sleep in a
Dmaj9 B♭dim7 Bm7 Em7 E6
cot or kay - ak. Châ - teau or shack, I tag - a - long
A9 G/A A7 Dmaj9 D6
too. In the thick of a quick - sand, in the grip of a

Em11 G/A A7 Dmaj9 D6 G6 Dmaj9 D6
squid, I will gay as a lark go___ from Park Row___ to
F♯m7(♭5) B9 Em7
skid. No mat - ter the weath - er or
Gm6 D6/A B9
To Coda II
e - ven wheth - er he wants me to go. How's he
Em7 Fdim7 F♯m7 Fdim7 Em7 A7(♭9) D6
D.C. al Coda I
gon - na get rid___ of a tag - a - long kid?___

Coda I
D
A7sus
A7
Em7
A7
(George:) Par - is to Pe - ru,
D
Am6/C
B7
'round the world I flew.
Em7
A
D
B♭dim7
Bm
Stand - ing by or stand - ing back,
D/A
E7
A7
I was once a shad - ow too.

D A7sus A7 Em7 A7
Lon - don to Ma - drid,
D F♯m7(♭5) B7
lone - ly dreams I hid,
Em7 Gm6 D/A A B7
dreams one day she'd turn my way, and lo! She
D.S. 𝄋 al Coda II
E9 A7 D G/A A7
did, she did! (Lois:) In a rick - et - y

Coda II
Em7
Fdim7
Bm7/F♯
Lois: gon - na get rid, how's he gon - na get rid,
George: Why, bless her heart, she did! Yes,
Fdim7
Em7
A7
how's he gon - na get rid of a tag - a - long
thank the Lord, she did! She
D
E♭9(♯11)
D
kid?
did!

THE MUSIC IN MY HEART

Words and Music by
LEROY ANDERSON

Moderately
F Dm7 Gm7 B♭/C C7 F B♭6 F Cdim7 C7 C7(♯5)
mf
F Dm7 Gm7 B♭/C C7 F
Ev - 'ry time you come my way, an or - ches-tra in-side of me be-
Cm7 F7 B♭ Gm7(♭5) F/C C Dm7 G6
gins to play. Oh, can't you hear the mu - sic in my
C7sus C7 Am B♭6 Gm7 C7 F Dm7
heart? Ev - 'ry time I

Gm7 B♭/C C7 F Cm7 F7
hold your hand, I seem to hear the thun - der of a might - y band. Oh,
B♭ Gm7(♭5) F/C C Gm7 C7 F B♭6
can't you hear the mu - sic in my heart?
F Bm7(♭5) E7 Am Bm11 E7
It's just a sim - ple love song; it's
Am E7 Am
noth - ing you could call sym - phon - ic. And yet this sim - ple

Bm11 E7 Am F♯dim7 Gm7 C7
love song sounds much sweet - er than the phil - har - mon - ic. The
F Dm7 Gm7 B♭/C C7 F
song is real, the words are true; they try to tell you some - thing of my
Cm7 F7 B♭ Gm7(♭5) F/C C Gm7 C7
love for you. Oh, can't you hear the mu - sic in my
1.
F B♭6 F Cdim7 C7 C7(♯5)
heart?
2.
F B♭6 F
heart?

WHAT'S THE USE OF LOVE?

Words and Music by
LEROY ANDERSON

Moderately
D♭ E♭m7 A♭9sus A♭7 D♭ Fm E♭m7 A♭7sus A♭7
mf
D♭ Fm7 B♭7 E♭m7 G♭m(maj7) G♭6
What's the use of love when no one's a - round to go ro - manc - ing?
Fm7 Edim7 E♭m7 A♭9sus A♭7 D♭(9) B♭m7 E♭m7 A♭9sus A♭7
When you're a - lone, what's the use of love?

D♭ Fm7 B♭7 E♭m7 G♭m(maj7) G♭6
What's the use of love when you sit and watch the oth-ers danc-ing?
Fm7 Edim7 E♭m7 A♭9sus A♭7 C♭13(♯11) B♭7
Out on your own, what's the use of love? There must be
B♭7(♭9)/E♭ E♭m E♭m7 A♭7 D♭dim7 G♭/D♭ D♭ B♭7
some-one near, some-one dear who's lone-ly, too, feel-ing the
B♭7(♭9)/E♭ E♭m G♭6 E♭m7 A♭13
way I do. If love is a dream, why can't it come true?

Db Fm7 Bb7 Ebm7 Gbm(maj7) Gb6
Stars may shine a - bove, but e - ven the stars_ are not en - tranc - ing.
Fm7 Edim7 Ebm7 Ab9sus Ab7
1. Db Fm
When you're a - lone,_ what's the use of love?
Ebm7 Ab7sus Ab7
2. Db Gb6 Db
love?_

THIS LOVELY WORLD

(from "Scarlett O'Hara")

Lyrics by
OGDEN NASH

Music by
LEROY ANDERSON

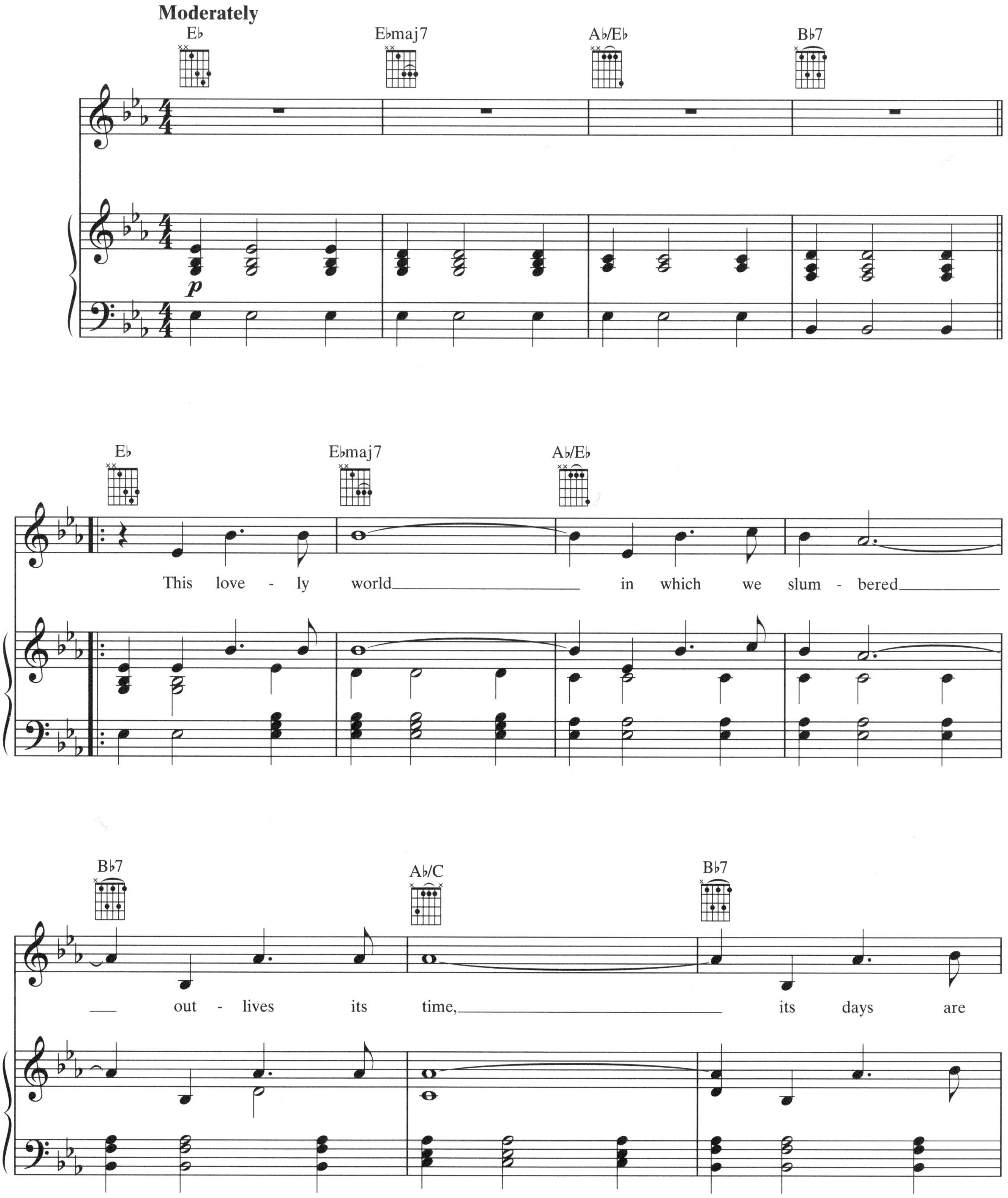
Moderately
E♭
E♭maj7
A♭/E♭
B♭7
p
E♭
E♭maj7
A♭/E♭
This love - ly world in which we slum - bered
B♭7
A♭/C
B♭7
out - lives its time, its days are

E♭
Cm
Gm
num - bered.
Our world must pass
Cm
Gm
Cm
like breath and glass.
The joys we
F13
F7
B♭7
shared de - part.
rall.
E♭
E♭maj7
A♭/B♭
This love - ly world
fades in - to
a tempo

B♭7
A♭/B♭
B♭7
fa - ble, like Ro - land's horn and Ar - thur's
E♭7
A♭
Cm
ta - ble. So falls the sky, but you and
F7
E♭/B♭
B♭13
B♭7
1. E♭
I will face it heart to heart.
rit.
a tempo
p
Fm/E♭
2. E♭
heart.
8vb